JAZZ**GUITAR**
CHORDCREATIVITY

A Complete Guide to Mastering Jazz Guitar Chords Anywhere on the Fretboard

TIM**PETTINGALE**

FUNDAMENTAL**CHANGES**

Jazz Guitar Chord Creativity

A Complete Guide to Mastering Jazz Guitar Chords Anywhere on the Fretboard

ISBN: 978-1-78933-152-3

Published by **www.fundamental-changes.com**

Copyright © 2019 Tim Pettingale

Edited by Joseph Alexander

www.fundamental-changes.com

Twitter: @guitar_joseph

Over 10,000 fans on Facebook: **FundamentalChangesInGuitar**

Instagram: **FundamentalChanges**

For over 350 Free Guitar Lessons with Videos Check Out

www.fundamental-changes.com

The audio for this book was recorded with an Eastman AR380CE-HB John Pisano signature model guitar. Cover image copyright: Eastman Music Company, used by permission.

www.eastmanguitars.com

Contents

Introduction

After a few years of playing rock, soul and funk I eventually discovered a passion for jazz and began listening to many of the masters – especially Joe Pass, Wes Montgomery, Pat Martino and Jim Hall. Coming from a self-taught background, I read, listened and played as much as I could and made some progress, but eventually it became apparent that I needed expert input from a teacher.

There wasn't a lack of information available – my dilemma was knowing exactly *what* I should study to become a better jazz guitarist. Sometimes it takes a good teacher to look at your playing and identify the gaps that need addressing, and I was fortunate to find one in legendary jazz educator Adrian Ingram.

It quickly became apparent that I only knew chord voicings in certain predictable areas of the neck. I could jump between these, but what about the no-man's land in between?

It was then that I began to study how to map chords across the entire fretboard, so that no area was out of bounds and I could use the full range of the instrument. This is a lifetime's work, but in this book, I've put together a creative method for jazz guitarists who want to quickly improve the practical application of their chord knowledge in a musical context.

Here you'll learn:

- How to play major, minor, dominant and half-diminished chords in multiple positions that span the range of the guitar neck

- How to connect those chords together in ii V I sequences in "zones" on the neck

- How to play chord sequences "vertically", combining voices and using the full range of the instrument to create beautiful, melodic comping ideas

By the end of this book you'll be playing jazz guitar chords in a much more melodic and interesting way. This will make you a better accompanist and give you many more options when playing with other musicians. This method will also feed into your solo chord-melody playing if that's an area you'd like to improve.

There will be a few neat substitution ideas thrown in along the way and, most importantly, you'll apply this knowledge to the changes of a couple of well-known jazz standards. Everything we learn *has* to be put to use in a practical setting, otherwise we don't truly absorb it.

The ideas in this book are designed to open up the fretboard, so you'll never be stuck playing in a few limited areas. I hope it will inspire you to come up with your own creative musical ideas.

Enjoy your playing,

Tim

Get the Audio

The audio files for this book are available to download for free from **www.fundamental-changes.com.** The link is in the top right-hand corner. Simply select this book title from the drop-down menu and follow the instructions to get the audio.

We recommend that you download the files directly to your computer, not to your tablet, and extract them there before adding them to your media library. You can then put them on your tablet, iPod or burn them to CD. On the download page there is a help PDF and we also provide technical support via the contact form.

For over 350 Free Guitar Lessons with Videos Check out:

www.fundamental-changes.com

Twitter: **@guitar_joseph**

Over 10,000 fans on Facebook: **FundamentalChangesInGuitar**

Instagram: **FundamentalChanges**

Chapter One – One Essential Chord Principle

One of the things that makes the guitar such an accessible instrument is the fact that we can learn chords in easy, memorable patterns. Over time, however, the same thing that helped us learn so quickly can become a barrier to progress. Guitar players love patterns and working in boxes, so when we see a particular chord written on a piece of music, it's all too easy to reach for a familiar shape. I had a breakthrough when I realised that certain shapes could be used for multiple purposes, thus opening up my harmonic options. This is a large topic in itself, but in this chapter, we'll look at a couple of "transferable" shapes which are particularly useful for jazz guitar.

One of the most common shapes for the major 7th chord that appears everywhere in jazz is illustrated below (Gmaj7). Jazz guitarists tend to learn this shape early on, as it falls naturally under the fingers and just sounds good.

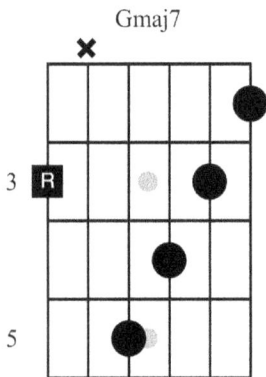

Gmaj7

Played in position 3, a bass note on the low E string is generally added, played with the thumb over the top of the neck. The low G bass helps set the sound of the chord in harmonic context for the listener.

If we replace the bass note with a different one, however, leaving all the other notes the same, the context of the chord changes. The diagram below shows the effect of changing the G bass note to an E.

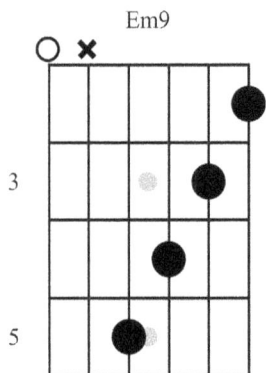

Em9

Notice that the chord is now called Em9. Before we examine what has happened, let's apply one more transformation. The next diagram shows the effect of changing the bass note from an E to an A. Now we call the chord A13.

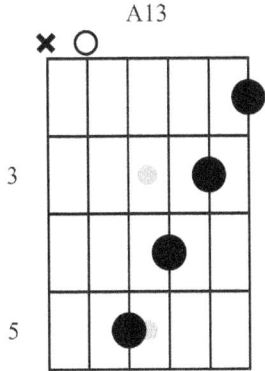

A13

Let's see what's going on. The Gmaj7 voicing in the first diagram has the following notes/intervals:

G	G	B	D	F#
Root	Root an octave higher	3rd	5th	7th

The Em9 voicing in this position has the following notes/intervals:

E	G	B	D	F#
Root	b3	5th	b7	9th

If we remove the bass notes of these chords, we are left with a stack of *identical* notes. Our ears will interpret these notes differently, depending on the context in which they are played:

Gmaj7:	G (root)	B (3rd)	D (5th)	F# (7th)
Em9:	G (b3)	B (5th)	D (b7)	F# (9th)

Notice that both chords contain the most important intervals that define their chord type – the 3rd, 5th and 7th.

Now let's examine the A13 chord. Essentially, a thirteenth is a seven-note chord, but for practical reasons (especially on the guitar with a limited number of fingers) certain notes are left out. The full version of A13 contains the following notes/intervals:

A	C#	E	G	B	D	F#
Root	3rd	5th	b7	9th	11th	13th

The A13 voicing in our example has the following notes/intervals:

A	G	B	D	F#
Root	b7	9th	11th	13th

Normally, when played on guitar, an A13 chord consists of the notes A (root), C# (3rd), G (b7), and F# (13th). The 5th, 9th and 11th intervals are generally omitted. So, what we have here is an *unusual* A13 voicing, but it's still an A13.

How can we use this concept in our playing?

If we think differently about this chord voicing, we get three chords for the price of one. We have one simple shape that can function as a major, minor or dominant chord, depending on the context. Here is a visual comparison of all three chords, without bass notes, highlighting the intervals.

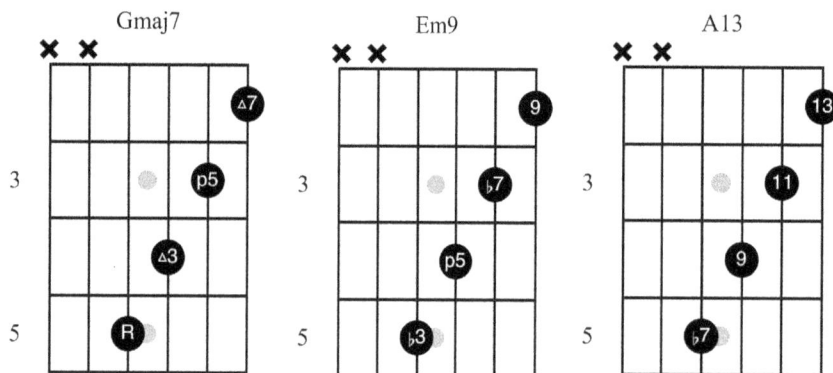

The chords are identical, but the *context* in which they are used will tell the listener what flavour of chord they are hearing.

Now, when you see "Em9" written in a piece of music, you can play this "Gmaj7" voicing and it will sound great – it contains all the same notes.

Let this information sink in for a moment. It means that whenever you see a major 7th chord, you can substitute a rootless minor 9th chord in its place and it will sound great, and vice versa. Let's put this concept to work right away and play a ii V I progression in the key of D Major using this chord shape.

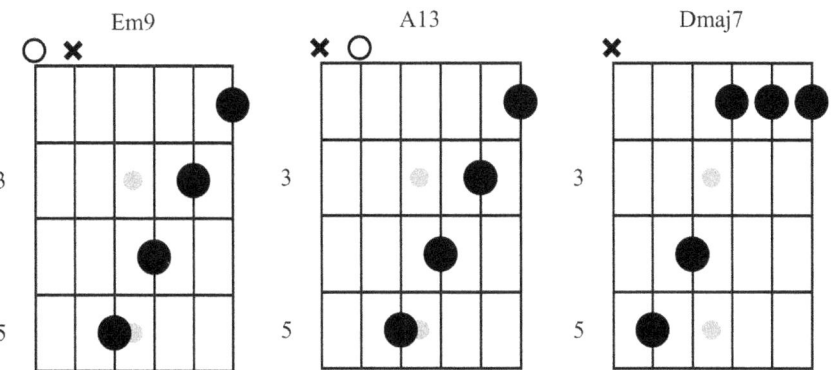

Example 1a

Are there any other useful chord shapes to which we can apply this principle?

If we strip away the root notes of a chord then yes, there are many examples of simple shapes that can be interpreted as different chords because of common notes. For the purpose of this book, however, I'll show you two more shapes that are particularly useful in a jazz context.

Major 6/minor 7 shapes

Simple major 6th chord shapes share the same notes as minor 7th chords. G6, for instance, has all the same notes as Em7 when played using the simple four-note voicings below. Therefore, they can be used interchangeably.

G6:	G (root)	B (3rd)	D (5th)	E (6th)
Em7:	E (root)	G (b3)	B (5th)	D (b7)

The following chord grids show the two most useful shapes to use and compare the respective intervals:

G6   Em7

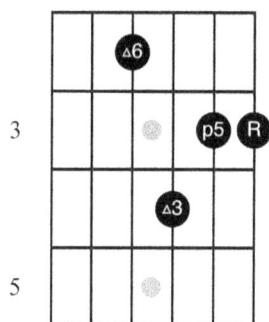 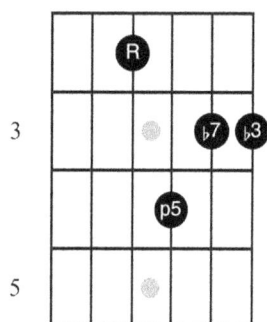

G6   Em7

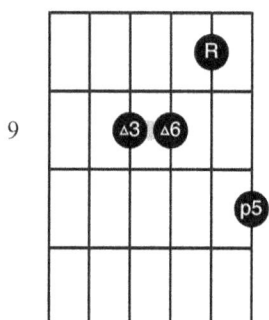 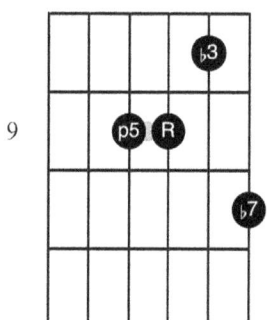

Remember these shapes, as they will crop up frequently in different guises.

In the next chapter we're going to begin the process of "mapping" chord shapes across the fretboard in order to break away from playing familiar shapes in safe areas of the neck. The aim is to become fluent at playing chords everywhere on the fretboard with no dead spots. You'll find this technique of multi-purpose chord shapes very useful in achieving full coverage of the neck.

Chapter Two – Breaking Out of Boxes

In this chapter you'll begin the journey of mapping chord shapes across the neck and learning how they fit together. To make this task easier and achieve maximum coverage of the guitar neck, you'll incorporate the interchangeable chord principle learnt in the previous chapter.

All the examples are based on a ii V I progression in the key of D Major: Em7 – A7 – Dmaj7. We will map each chord separately and spend some time playing through the chord shapes, so that the patterns really begin to sink in. Once you've learnt all the shapes for a particular chord across the neck, you can use them whenever you need to comp on a single chord for several bars. Nothing here is simply a boring exercise.

Important caveat! There are lots of "chord systems" out there on the Internet and some great interactive apps that can assist with the mapping of scales and chords. Knowing every possible permutation of a chord, however, doesn't give you any insight into where and how to use it. Here I don't cover every conceivable option, but the ideas presented should serve you well in practical playing situations, such as in a band setting or as a solo accompanist.

Now, let's break down the ii V I sequence in D Major, chord by chord.

The ii chord

E minor chord shapes – Set 1

Here is a sequence of E minor chords that span the range of the neck. These particular shapes have been chosen for their suitability for comping with a rhythm section. In a typical small-group jazz setting, you'll often find yourself playing with a bass player and/or or a pianist. Piano chords and guitar chords occupy a similar sonic space, so things can quickly become muddy if both musicians are playing full chords in a similar register.

Similarly, the continuous walking bassline of jazz means that the bassist has the bottom end well covered. For this reason, the chord shapes here are nearly all voiced on the top 4 strings of the guitar and should produce less mud and more clarity.

Play through these chords in order, ascending, several times. Then practise the sequence descending.

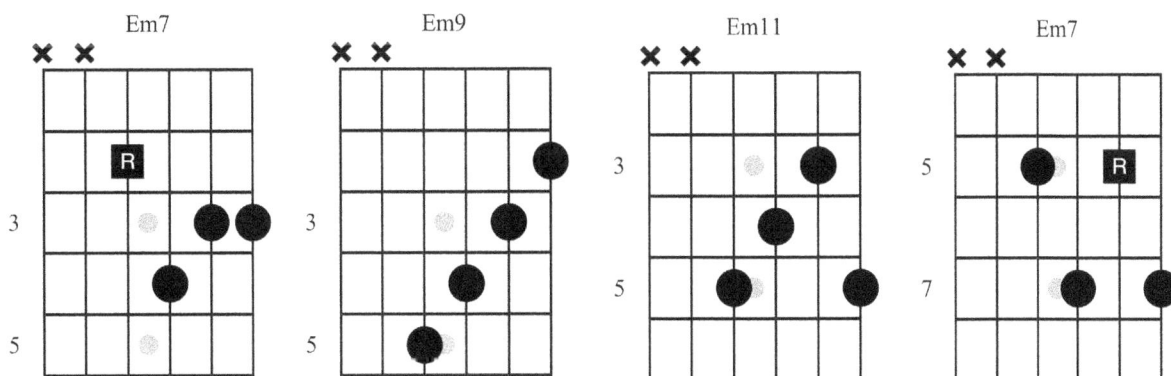

Em11   Em7   Em11   Em9 (no root)

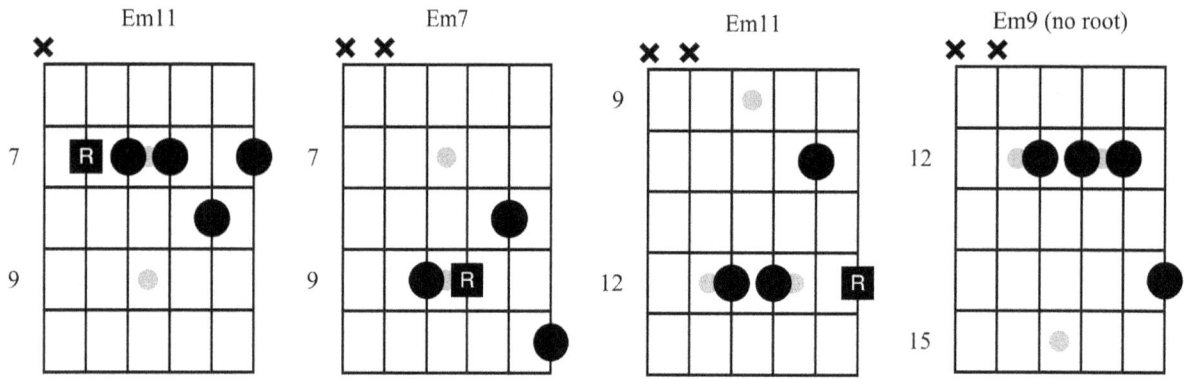

Play the chords ascending and descending and allow a bar for each chord.

Example 2a

Em7   Em9   Em11   Em7

Em11   Em7   Em11   Em9

Example 2b "pairs up" chords and alternates between them while descending the neck. The pattern ends when there are no more chords to alternate between! This will test how well you've learnt the shapes and how smoothly you can change between them. The audio examples here at set at a reasonable 80bpm, but by all means practise these out of tempo until you've mastered all the shapes, then play along to the backing track.

Example 2b

Now, mix up the chords and play them out of sequence. Put your metronome on and concentrate on playing a strong rhythm that includes accents. Focus on any chord voicings you like the sound of, but make sure you play in several zones of the neck. Here's one simple example to get you started.

Example 2c

Make sure to spend enough time with these chord shapes – especially those that are new to you – and set aside practice time to become fluent at playing them in sequence as well as picking out individual voicings.

E minor chord shapes – Set 2

This second set of E minor shapes is intended to be used when playing solo jazz guitar, accompanying a singer in a duo setting, or playing in a trio with guitar, drums and bass. This time, bass notes are allowed as the guitar is the main harmonic instrument.

The focus here is on finding lush sounding minor voicings that work across the range of the neck, and less on producing a playable sequence. In due course, we'll put these shapes to work in a ii V I sequence.

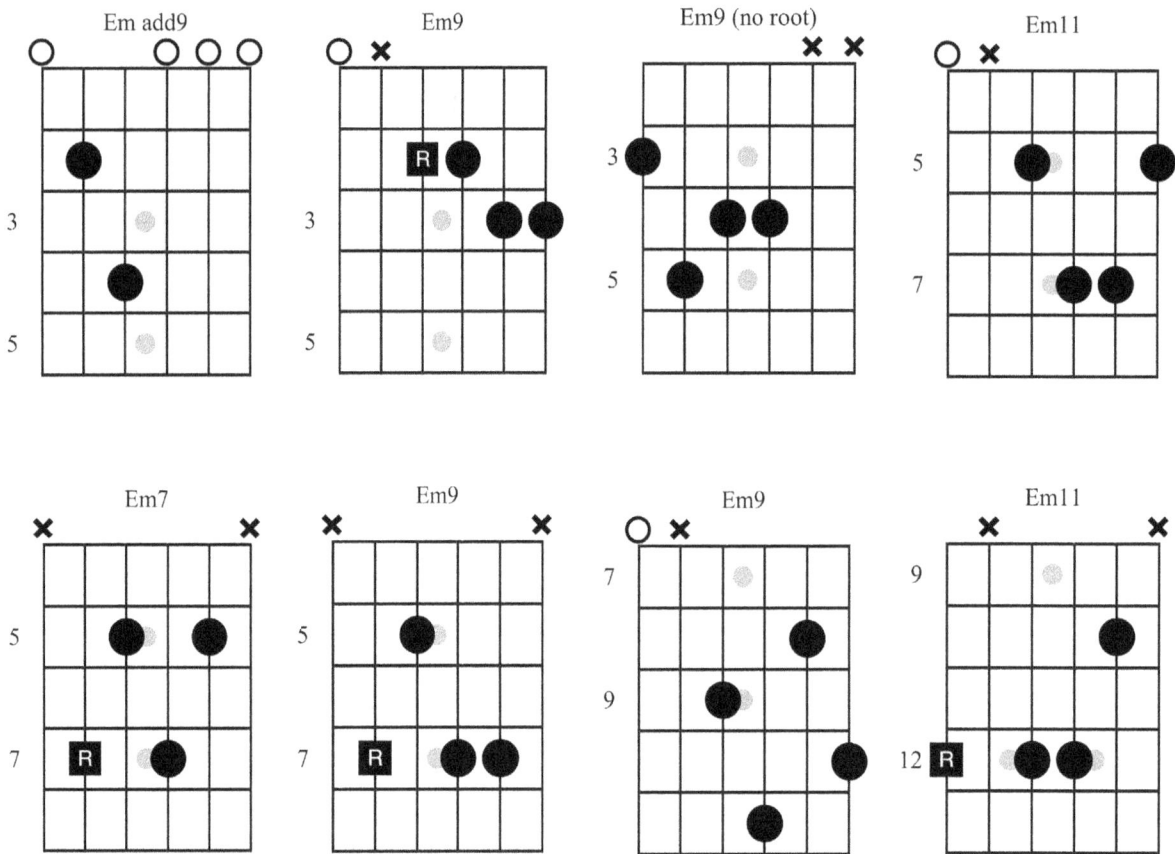

In Example 2d the chords are played in sequence for one bar each. As before, practise them ascending and descending.

NB: although the chords are written as a single strum below, experiment with sounding the low E first, then strumming the rest of the chord.

Example 2d

The V Chord

A Dominant 7 chord shapes – Set 1

Now we'll look at the V chord in the ii V I progression (A7) and follow the same process. Set 1's voicings are to be played vertically on the fretboard in sequence and are designed for a band setting.

A9   A9sus   A7   A9sus(13)

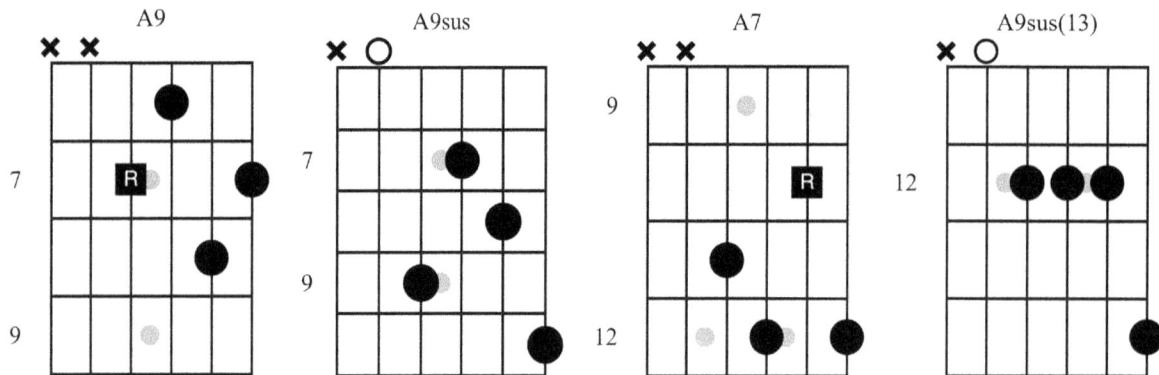

Play the chords ascending and descending and allow one bar for each chord.

Example 2e

Now pair up alternate chords as before and play them descending. Practise until the changes become smooth.

Example 2f

Now, mix up the voicings and pick out your favourites to comp against your metronome.

Example 2g

A Dominant 7 chord shapes – Set 2

Set 2 of the dominant chord shapes are for use when the guitar is the main harmonic instrument. There are more shapes this time, because I've included several different versions of the common A7 shape at the 5th fret.

A13b9   A9 (no root)   A7   A13

A13b9   A7#5   A7b9   A7#11

A13   A7   A9   A13

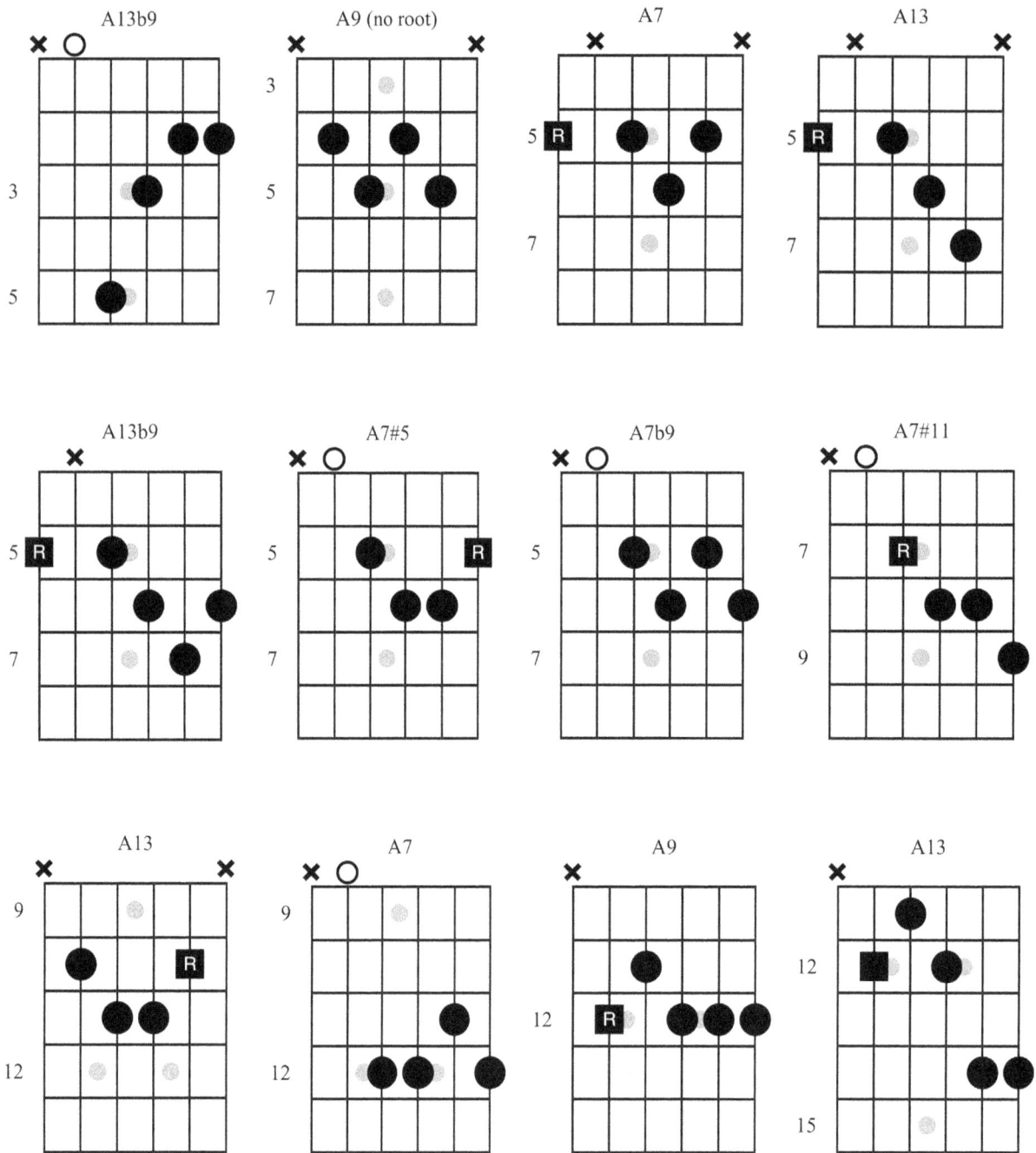

Practise these chord shapes as illustrated in Example 2h below.

Example 2h

A13♭9　　　A9 no root　　　A7　　　A13

A13♭9　　　A7♯5　　　A7♭9　　　A7♯11

A13　　　A7　　　A9　　　A13

The I Chord

D Major chord shapes – Set 1

Finally, work through the following D Major chord shapes using the same process. Here are the Set 1 vertical voicings.

Dmaj7　　　Dmaj7　　　D6　　　Dmaj7

Dmaj7   **Dmaj7**   **D6(9)**   **Dmaj7**

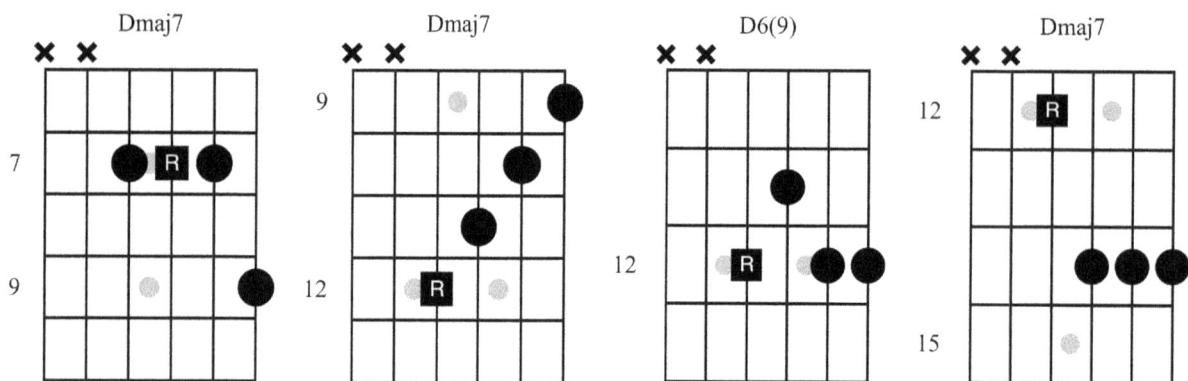

Practise these chords ascending and descending.

Example 2i

Dmaj7	Dmaj7	D6	Dmaj7

```
        1              2              3              4
TAB     2              2              5              5
        2              2              3              7
        2              2              4              6
        0              4              4              7
                       5                             5
```

Dmaj7	Dmaj7	D6(9)	Dmaj7

```
        5              6              7              8
TAB     9              9              12             14
        7              10             12             14
        7              11             11             14
        7              12             12             12
```

Now pair up alternate chords as shown in Example 2j.

Example 2j

Finally, mix up the voicings and pick out your favourites to comp with. Here's one approach for you.

Example 2k

D Major chord shapes – Set 2

Now, here are the Set 2 chord shapes for use when you want to play a fuller accompaniment.

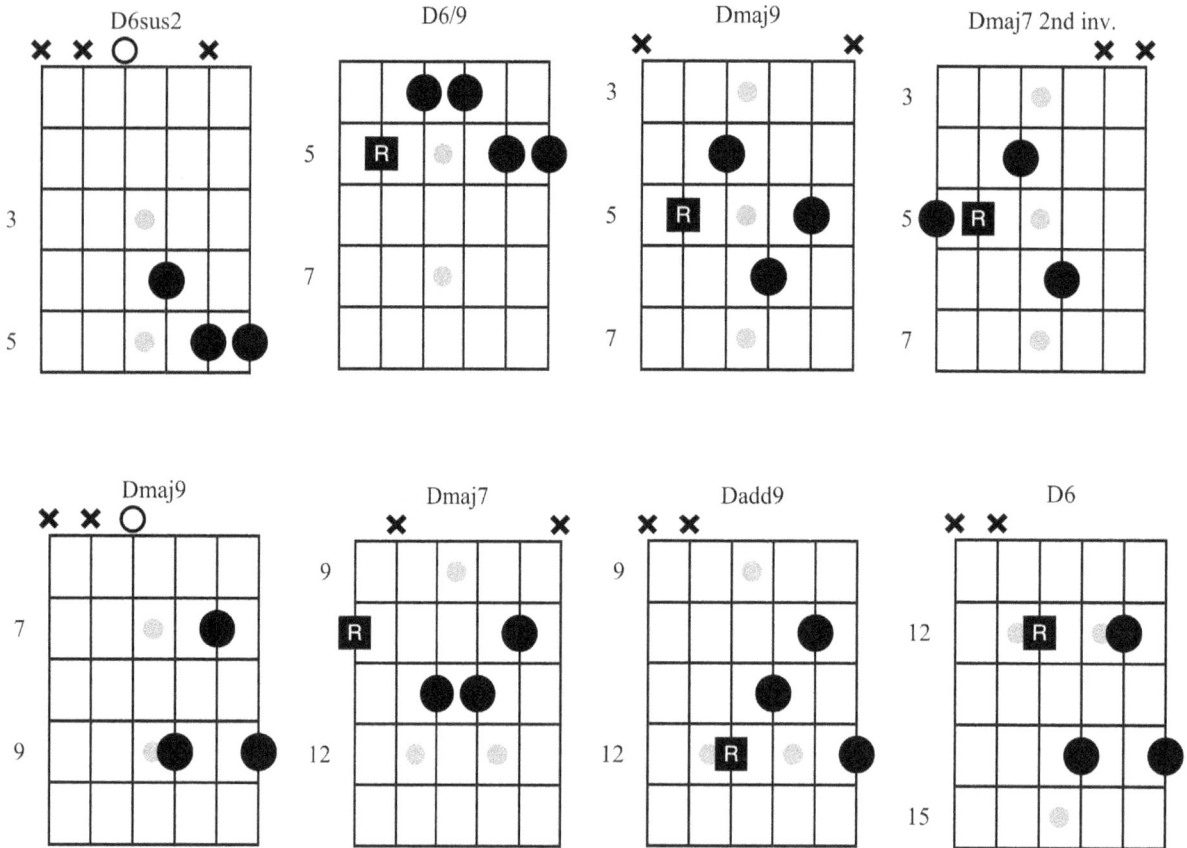

Practise these chord shapes as shown in Example 2h, setting your metronome to a comfortable pace.

Example 21

In the next chapter we'll combine all the chord shapes we've looked at so far into useful ii V I sequences.

Chapter Three – Expanding Your Harmonic Choices

So far, we've looked at how to cover the fretboard by mapping chords across the neck. The more you practise these vertical chord sequences, the more you'll begin to break away from playing chords in your familiar, go-to positions.

The next step to achieving freedom across the range of the fretboard is to learn to combine the chord shapes in "zones" on the guitar. You'll play the ii V I sequence within in a limited range of frets, which will assist with memorising the different chord shapes, while giving you something meaningful and melodic to play.

The chord combinations here have been carefully chosen to ensure the chord voicings complement each other well. By the end of this chapter you'll be able to play a ii V I progression in the same key in multiple areas of the fretboard, and you'll have many more options at your fingertips when you are comping.

Once you are fluent at playing these patterns in zones, in the next chapter you'll learn some great ways of freely moving the length of the fretboard to play ii V I patterns combining multiple shapes in different zones.

This chapter has lots of examples, so I recommend you work through them methodically. The zones are arranged from low to high, so you'll gradually ascend the fretboard.

I've provided chord grids and notation/TAB for each sequence. You can also refer to the free audio to hear how each example sounds.

For the purposes of this chapter we'll play one bar each of Em7 and A7, and two bars of Dmaj7:

| Em7 | A7 | Dmaj7 | % |

Zone 1 – Frets 0-3

Example 3a

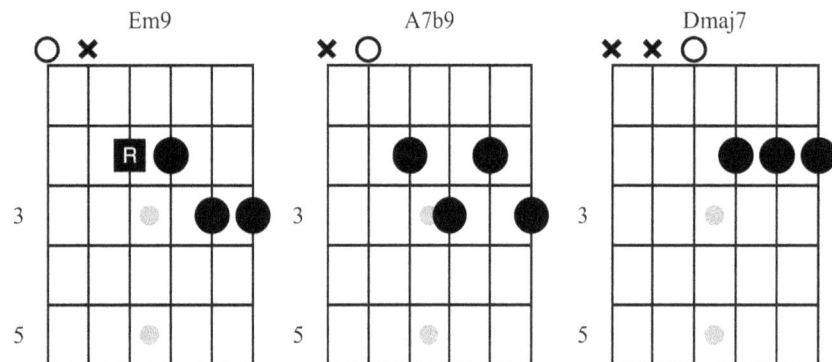

Em9 **A7♭9** **Dmaj7**

Whenever you're able include open strings in a voicing, you should, as it creates a harmonically richer sound.

Example 3b

Em add9   A13   Dmaj7

Em add9 **A13** **Dmaj7**

Zone 2 – Frets 3-5

Here's the very open sounding ii V I that uses the maj7 substitution idea discussed in Chapter One.

Example 3c

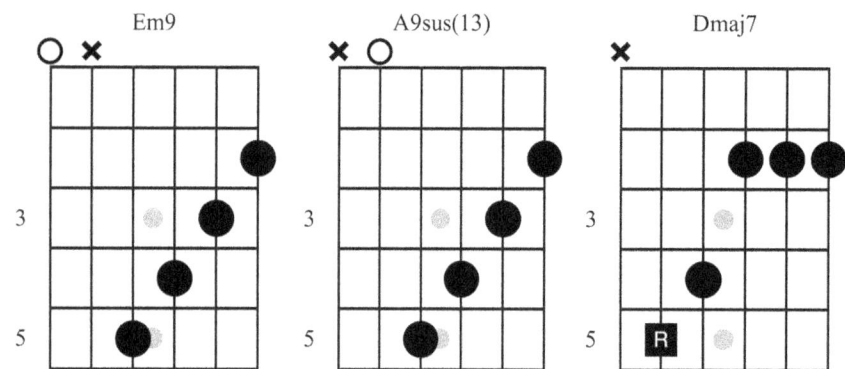

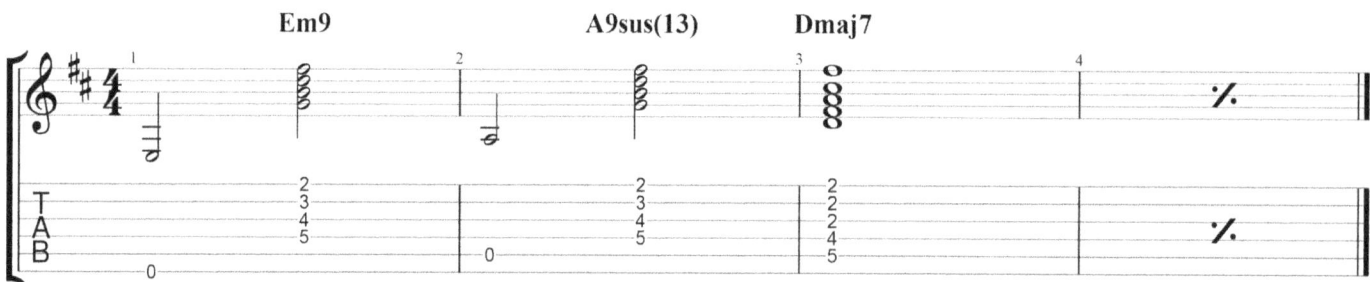

The next example has an unusual, bright sounding D6(9) voicing for chord I.

Example 3d

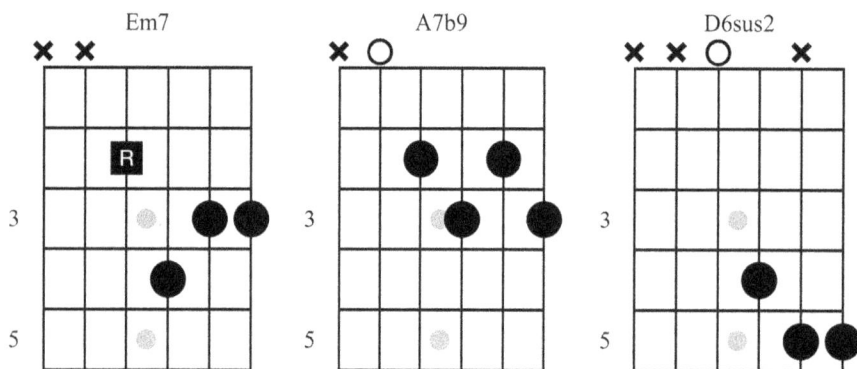

A slight adjustment to the transferable maj7 shape from Chapter One creates the tense but beautiful A13b9 chord for chord V. (Two notes of the original stacked maj7 are lowered by a semitone, on the G and B strings).

Example 3e

Here is an unusual combination of chords, beginning with an Em9 that has no root note and provides a rich accompaniment for a vocalist. The low, close voicings have a real warmth to them.

Example 3f

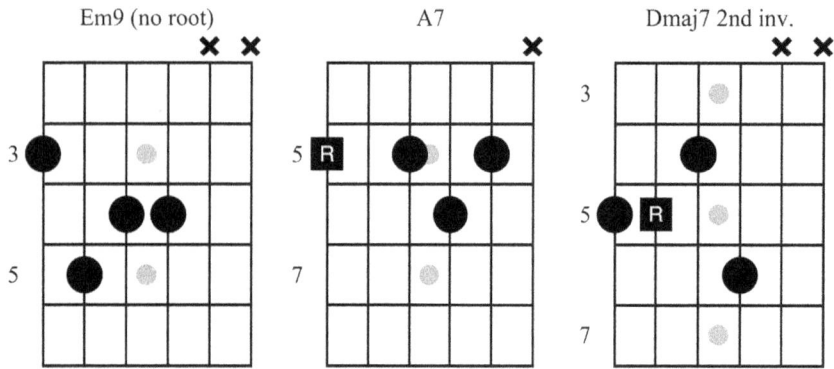

By way of contrast, here is a light, airy way of playing the progression. (NB: I know this is supposed to be the 3-5 fret zone, and this sequence creeps higher, but it just felt like it wanted to ascend, and I think you'll agree it sounds nice!)

Example 3g

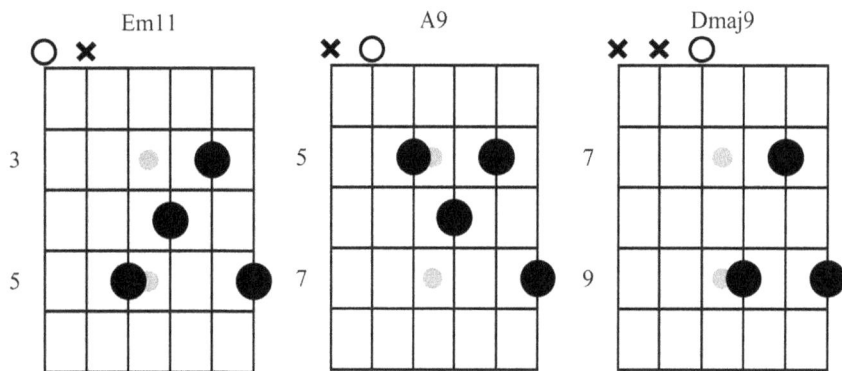

Em11   A9   Dmaj9

Zone 3 – Frets 5-7

Example 3h has always been one of my personal go-to sequences. It's an economical and good-sounding arrangement of the chords. Personally, I work hard to avoid playing this by default and you should do the same with your own habitual chord voicings.

Example 3h

Em9   A13   Dmaj7

Em9   A13   Dmaj7

Example 3i

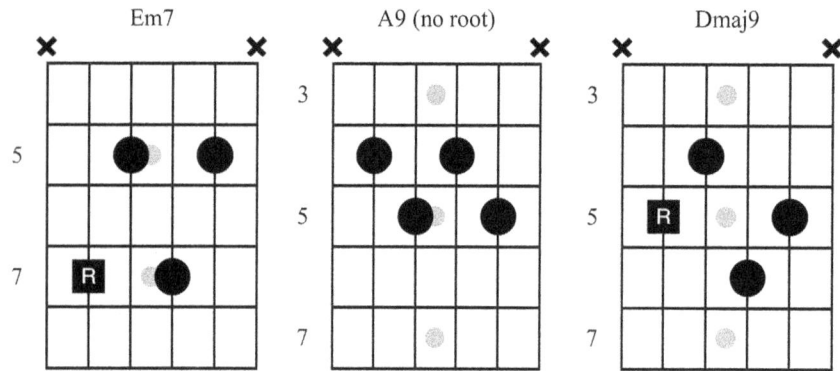

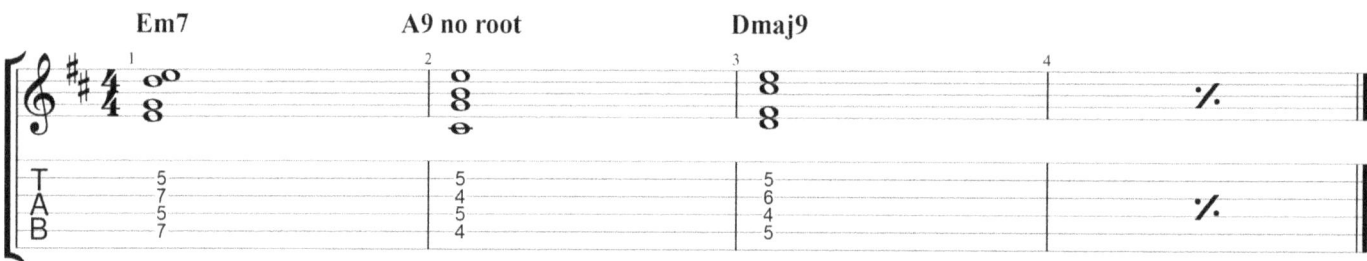

The next example is arranged so that the A note (high E string, fifth fret) rings out on every chord as a kind of pedal tone. For ease of playing, I recommend you bar the top four strings with your index finger at the fifth fret and play the Em11 and A7#5 like bar chords. Play the open E and A string bass notes with your thumb.

Example 3j

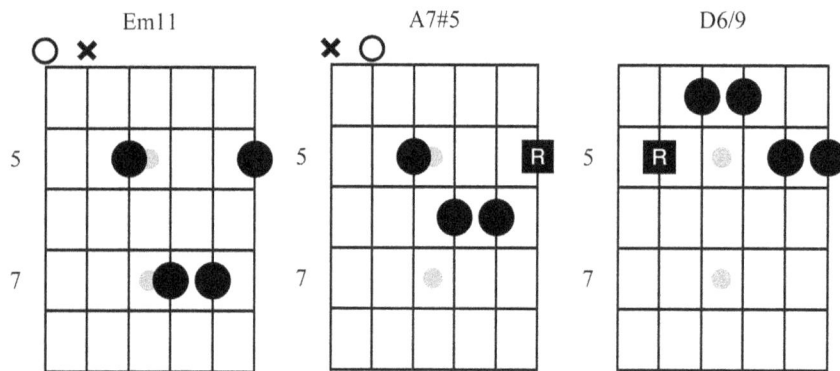

Em11   A(#5   D6(9)

A different take on Example 3h has an A13b9 chord instead of a straight A13. The 13b9 chord creates a lot of tension and strongly wants to resolve.

Example 3k

Em9   A13b9   Dmaj7

Em9   A13♭9   Dmaj7

Small movements can be very effective on guitar. Here you can see that lowering two notes by a semitone turns the Em7 shape into A7b9. These chords are followed by a D6/9, giving a nice chromatic descending note on the high E string that provides a strong sense of movement.

Example 3l

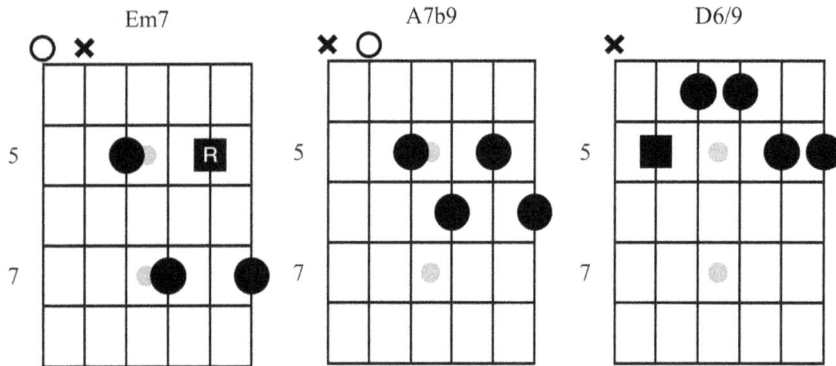

Zone 4 – Frets 7-9

Playing in the 7-9 fret zone of the fretboard, you can access chord shapes that will work well if you often play with a pianist. We're getting away from the middle register of the guitar, which occupies a similar frequency range to the piano, and these airy sounding chords won't make things sound muddy.

Example 3m is a good example of this. If you're playing with a pianist, or just a double bassist who is holding down the bottom end, you can leave out the bass notes.

Notice that the Dmaj7 chord looks like a Bm9 without the B bass note. This is another version of the interchangeable maj7 – m9 chord voicings discussed earlier.

Dmaj7 chord construction = D, F#, A and C#

Bm9 chord construction (leaving out the root) = D, F#, A and C#

Example 3m

Em7   A7b9   Dmaj7

Em7   A7♭9   Dmaj7

Example 3n

Em11   A13   Dmaj7 (no root)

The Em9 shape in Example 3o is one of my favourites but can be tricky to finger. Play through this example slowly until you can switch between the chords smoothly.

NB: Although the chords are notated played straight, it can be nice to arpeggiate them.

Example 3o

Example 3p is another example that highlights the effectiveness of moving one or two notes to create a new chord voicing in the same position. The transition from A7#11 to Dmaj7 is achieved by lowering the notes on the G and B strings a semitone.

Example 3p

Em11   A7#11   Dmaj7

Zone 5 – Frets 9-12

In this example, the movement from A13 to Dmaj7 is achieved by moving a single note across a string.

Example 3q

Here is a way of moving from Em11 to A7 by moving just one note in the chord voicing.

Example 3r

Zone 6 – Frets 12-15

Example 3s

Here is one final example. You could choose to drop the lowest notes in the A9 and D6 chords and play open A and D bass notes instead.

Example 3t

I suggest playing through each of these sequences in this chapter multiple times as you gradually ascend the fretboard. This will help to lock in the shapes and embed the sound in your ears.

Now that we've played the chords in zones on the neck, it's time to develop greater fretboard independence by mixing and matching shapes that span a much greater range.

Chapter Four – Vertical Chord Playing

If you study the solo guitar playing or comping of Joe Pass, Martin Taylor, George Benson, Kurt Rosenwinkel and other greats, and observe how they move around the fretboard, you'll notice that they tend to play *vertically* more than *horizontally*. They all use multiple voicings of a chord to span the fretboard. This adds momentum to their musical statements, and also helps to create achieve different tones and timbres.

To achieve the same kind of freedom, in this chapter you'll learn:

- Multiple examples of beautiful ways to connect chords in ii V I sequences that move vertically, spanning the range of the neck

- How to embellish chord connections so they become "chord-phrases" in their own right

Let's begin to put together some vertical voicings. Sometimes I'll use multiple voicings of one chord and only one of each of the others in the ii V I sequence. My aim is to mix things up and keep the focus on being musical.

As in the previous chapter, we'll play one bar each of Em7 and A7, and two bars of Dmaj7:

| Em7 | A7 | Dmaj7 | % |

What follows is multiple ways to play the ii V I sequence using the chord shapes and connections you've learnt so far. Practise each of these sequences until the chord changes become smooth and flowing.

Example 4a allows two beats per chord for the E minor and A dominant chords.

Example 4a

The next example uses three E minor shapes in the first bar, then allows the A dominant and D Major chords to sustain.

Example 4b

Here's a sequence that changes chord every two beats to create continuous movement through the progression.

Example 4c

Em11   Em7   A9   A7#5   Dmaj7   Dmaj7   Dmaj7   D6

The descending idea in Example 4d shows how it's possible to span a huge range of the fretboard using this concept. The Em9 chord at the beginning, and the Dmaj7 at the end, both have an F# as the top note in the voicing, 12 frets apart.

Example 4d

Em9 (no root)   Em7   Em7   A7b9   Dmaj7

Em9 no root   Em7   Em7   A7b9   Dmaj7

Here's another two-beats-per-chord idea that spans frets 5-12.

Example 4e

Example 4f shifts the focus to the A dominant chord this time and takes advantage of the movable nature of the A7b9 chord. The idea spans a wide range of the guitar neck.

Example 4f

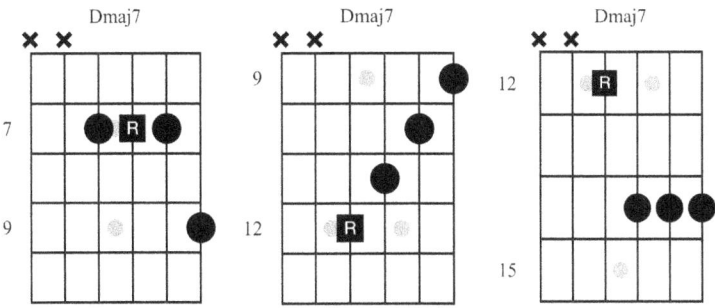

In Example 4g, a descending pattern of E minor voicings is played, one beat per chord. Thereafter each chord plays for two beats. This idea descends, then ascends through D major voicings.

Example 4g

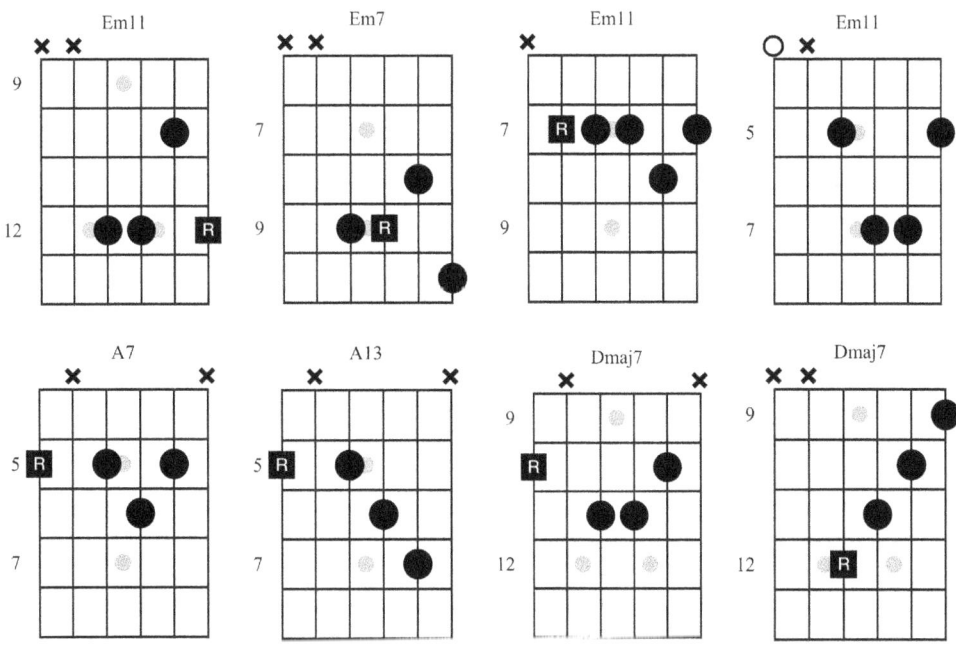

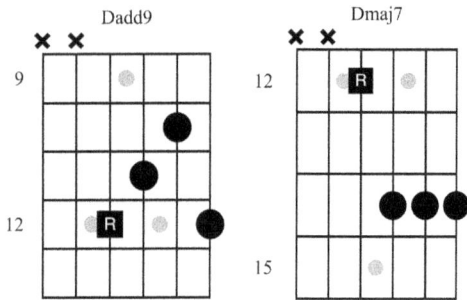

Dadd9   Dmaj7

Em11 Em7 Em11 Em11   A7   A13   Dmaj7   Dmaj7   Dadd9   Dmaj7

```
      12    10    7     7                            9       12      14
      10     8    8     7     5     7     10    10    10      10      14
      12     9    7     7     6     6     11    11    11      11      14
      12     9    7     7     5     5     11    12    12      12      12
                        7                       10
                        0     5     5     10
```

Take time to play through the above examples until you can play the changes very smoothly and comfortably. The aim is to memorise the shapes as a musical sequence, and for the shapes to become second nature to you. As you work on them, you're building your chord vocabulary in a way you can instantly apply.

Decorating chord connections

Now we move on to look at how we can embellish our vertical chord connections to create pleasing melodic chord phrases. By this, I simply mean to reach for notes in the vicinity of the chord shape to create short melodic phrases. These simple movements can both enhance the chords and assist with connecting them together. It's not chord-melody playing as such but practising this approach will definitely feed into your solo guitar playing. You can also use these ideas for intros, outros or chord solos in accompaniment.

"Decorating" a chord sequence can be as simple as:

• Sliding into a chord from below

• Adding approach notes between chords

• Arpeggiating one chord in a sequence while all the others are strummed

• Altering or extending chords to add colour (for instance, changing a basic A7 chord in fifth position to A7#5 in the same position by raising one note)

These are all quite simple ideas that will enhance the chord progression, but as Joe Pass once said, "Why would you want to play anything hard?!" I hope the following licks will act as a stimulus for you to explore and discover your own.

The first example is based around position five and uses a pedal note between chords to create a simple melody. The Dmaj7 chord is played in positions five and seven to support the melodic line as it continues. All the notes are from the D Major scale.

Example 4h

In the next example, the Em7 chord in position seven is embellished with a chordal hammer-on as means of ascending to the Em9 shape in position twelve. Once in position twelve, I play the nearest voicings of A9 and Dmaj7.

Example 4i

The next idea spans a wide range of the fretboard. Starting at the twelfth fret, three E minor voicings descend the neck to "land" on the A dominant chord. Then, beginning with a straightforward open position Dmaj7, multiple major 7 shapes are used to ascend the neck to end where the line began.

Example 4j

In Example 4k I slide an Em11 shape in position seven up a tone and back. For the A dominant chord, I play an A13 in position five followed by an A7#5 chord. This is followed by familiar Dmaj7 and Dmaj9 chords.

Example 4k

The next example illustrates the kind of line Joe Pass often played, where he would hold down a simple chord shape with two fingers and use his free fingers to play a melodic line. The notes come from the D Major scale. When playing the line, be careful not to choke the chords. The strings that aren't required to play the melody should still be ringing to provide subtle support for the line.

Example 4l

Here's the same kind of idea applied to higher voicings.

Example 4m

Example 4n is played as fully strummed chords in the style of Wes Montgomery, punctuated by the occasional note. Wes often approached his solos in the same way: single lines, followed by octaves, followed by block chord riffs. This is the type of thing he might have played to maintain momentum in a solo.

Example 4n

Example 4o is a simple but elegant way of moving from one end of the neck to the other. It makes use of the movable nature of the A7b9 chord shape.

Example 4o

This idea uses both a chordal hammer-on and melody notes on an Em7 chord shape in position seven. The phrase acts as a springboard to launch further up the neck.

Example 4p

So far, the examples have been reasonably simple – to illustrate how effective it can be to decorate a chord sequence with one or two notes or a simple phrase. Here's a longer idea at a moderate tempo with three ii V I's back to back. It links together a number of the ideas covered so far.

Example 4q

How to practise this technique

To begin to develop your own chord phrases, use the chord sequences illustrated in Chapter Three as a starting point and see what embellishments you can add. You might come up with a simple phrase that connects the three chords, or other creative ways of decorating them. Here are a few examples to start you off.

Example 4r (based on Example 3e)

Example 4s (based on Example 3g)

Example 4t (based on Example 3h)

Example 4u (based on Example 3m)

Example 4v (based on Example 3p)

Now work on creating your own chord phrases from scratch. I recommend playing free time to begin with, while you are composing ideas. When you discover an idea you like, play it in tempo to a metronome and focus on playing the changes smoothly.

Chapter Five – Introducing Chord Substitutions

We have looked at how to:

- Map chords across the fretboard

- Play the ii V I progression in multiple zones on the neck

- Play vertical ii V I progressions that span the fretboard

- Embellish progressions with chord phrases

The next logical step to enhance your chord playing and to express more harmonically advanced ideas is to introduce chord substitutions.

If all the work we've done so far has been to "join the dots" between chords to achieve freedom on the guitar fretboard, then chord substitutions are the "dots between the dots"! You can use the following ideas to create tension and release, to connect together different zones of the fretboard, to vary your chord sequences, and ultimately to compose more challenging melodic lines.

We'll approach this material in the same way as previously, taking one substitution idea at a time. For each substitution there will be:

- Vertical chord shape sequences that include the substitution

- Embellished chord phrases which use the substitution

NB: For these examples I'm also adding a passing VI7 chord (B7) at the end of the progression to create a turnaround. The B7 chord naturally wants to resolve to Em7, so you can play the sequence continuously for practice purposes:

| Em7 | A7 | Dmaj7 | Dmaj7 B7 |

Keep referring back to this sequence as "home" as we gradually alter the changes below.

1. Tritone substitution #1

One of the most common devices in jazz is the tritone or flat five chord substitution. The dominant V chord in a progression is replaced by another dominant chord a b5 interval above it. The "tri" part of "tritone" refers to the three whole steps between the two chords. Our V chord is A7. Move up three whole steps on the guitar and you'll arrive at Eb7. If we analyse the A7 and Eb7 chords, we see they share the same 3rd and 7th intervals, but in reverse order.

The progression:

| Em7 | Eb7 | Dmaj7 | Dmaj7 B7 |

The chord shapes:

Every time you encounter a chord progression, think of it in terms of what you've learned so far: work at playing it in zones on the guitar neck; then work at playing it vertically, so you can roam the fretboard at will.

Look back at the chord patterns you've learnt so far and think about how the Eb7 chord can be incorporated. Here's a common way of adding in the b5 that falls easily on the guitar:

Example 5a

Now here is one way of incorporating the b5 chord into a vertical sequence.

Example 5b

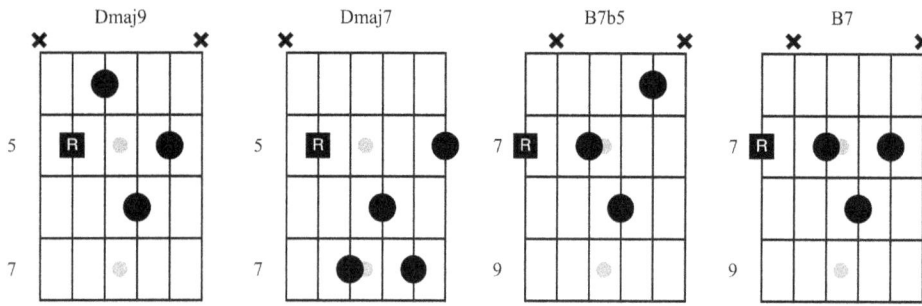

Example 5c uses a different set of chord shapes and adds decoration to create a melodic chord phrase.

Example 5c

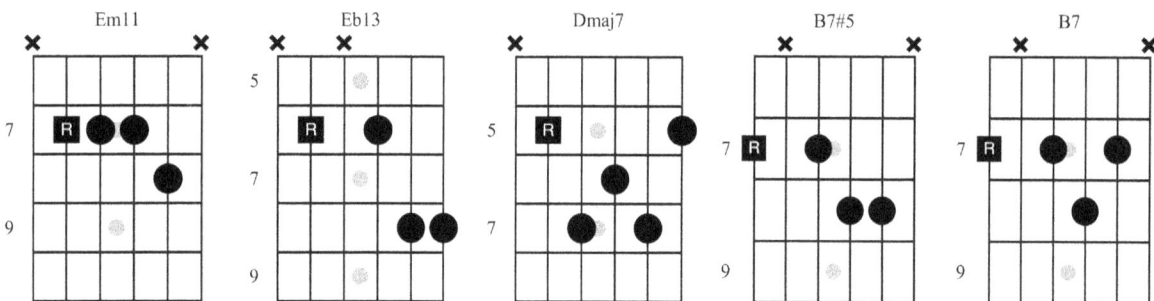

2. Tritone substitution #2

A major focus of bebop-style jazz is to add ii V sequences into chord progressions to enrich the harmony and therefore increase the melodic options for soloing. It has become common when reharmonizing jazz standards to treat a dominant chord as though it is a functional V chord and precede it with the ii chord from the same key.

Let's take the Eb7 chord from the previous example. Eb7 is the V chord in the key of Ab Major. Bb minor is the ii chord from that key. We can include both chords to alter the progression to this:

The progression:

| Em7 | Bbm9 Eb9 | Dmaj7 | Dmaj7 B7 |

This increases the movement in the progression, but the addition of the Bbm9 opens up another whole set of possible chord shapes.

We learnt in Chapter One that rootless minor 9 shapes are interchangeable with stacked major 7 shapes. A rootless Bm9 chord shape has all the same notes as a stacked Dbmaj7 chord. The two are interchangeable and, handily, Dbmaj7 is a semitone below the Dmaj7 chord we are heading towards. Therefore, we could express the tritone substitution like this:

| Em7 | Bbm9 Dbmaj7 | Dmaj7 | Dmaj7 B7 |

With a couple of simple steps, suddenly we've got lots of options at our fingertips. Here is one suggested route through these changes. During your practice sessions it's your mission to discover your own.

The chord shapes:

Example 5d

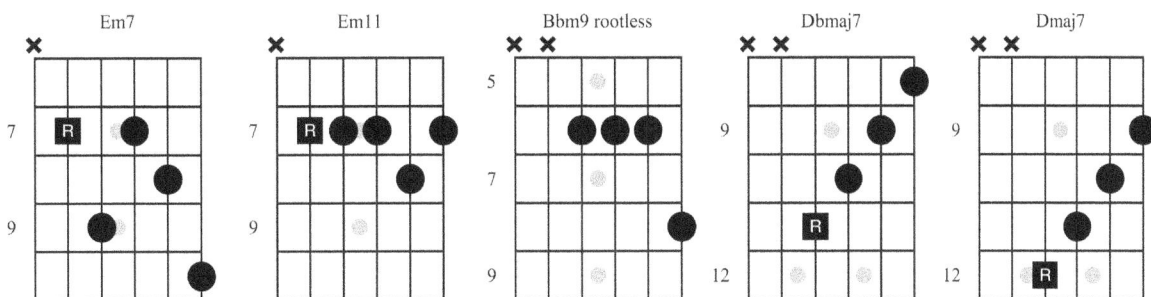

Now here is a chord phrase example based on these changes.

Example 5e

3. Major seventh b5 substitution

In Tritone example #1 we substituted a dominant 7th chord located a b5 above our original A7 chord to create this progression:

| Em7 | Eb7 | Dmaj7 | Dmaj7 B7 |

What if we changed the *quality* of that chord to a major 7th instead? Now we have:

The progression:

| Em7 | Ebmaj7 | Dmaj7 | Dmaj7 B7 |

This isn't considered a tritone in traditional harmony, as Ebmaj7 and A7 only have one note in common. Instead you could think of this as a chromatic approach chord – approaching the target Dmaj7 chord from a semitone above.

Here is one way to play these changes.

The chord shapes:

Example 5f

Em11   Em7   Cm9 no root   E♭maj7   Dmaj7   Dmaj7   B7♭9 no root

```
T|--7----10----10----6-----5-----9-----8----|
A|--8-----8-----8----8-----7-----7-----7----|
 |--7-----9-----8----7-----6-----7-----8----|
 |--7-----9-----8----8-----7-----7-----7----|
B|--7-----------------6-----5----------------|
```

Notice that I used the minor 9th/major 7th device above, first playing a rootless Cm9 followed by Ebmaj7.

This substitution has a dreamy quality to it and the tension of the Ebmaj7 chord begs to be resolved to Dmaj7. Here is an example of how you can develop this idea into a chord phrase.

Example 5g

Em7   Cm7   E♭maj7   Dmaj7   D7♭9

```
T|--7----10----10---8---6---8----5----5---7--10----9---7---8---7--|
A|--8-----8-----8-------8-------7----7-----------7-------7--------|
 |--7-----9-----8-------7-------6----6----------7-------8--------|
 |--7-----9-----8-------8-------7----7----------7-------7--------|
B|--7-----------------------------5----5--------------------------|
```

4. Major seventh b5 extended substitution

Once you begin to push the envelope of the standard ii V I progression, other rich harmonic choices come into view. So as not to become baffled by all these choices, it's best to play through the vanilla ii V I and add just *one* new flavour at a time. Work with that one concept until you've exhausted your ideas, then pick another flavour to experiment with. Gradually, these ideas will be absorbed into your playing and will feel like a natural part of your vocabulary.

This next version of the ii V I retains the Ebmaj7 from the previous example, but adds in an Abmaj7. Where on earth has Abmaj7 appeared from, you may wonder! This time I've added in a major 7th chord a b5 above Dmaj7 (Ab is a b5 above D).

The progression:

| Em7 | Ebmaj7 Abmaj7 | Dmaj7 | Dmaj7 B7 |

At first glance you may think this appears a bit "out there" but listen to how it sounds played in one zone of the neck. This arrangement could create interest when supporting another instrumentalist in a duo setting, or serve as an introduction for a vocalist.

The chord shapes:

Example 5h

Em11   Ebmaj7   Abmaj9   Dmaj7   Dmaj7   B13(b9)

Example 5i develops this substitution idea and uses different chord shapes to achieve a spacious, open sound.

Example 5i

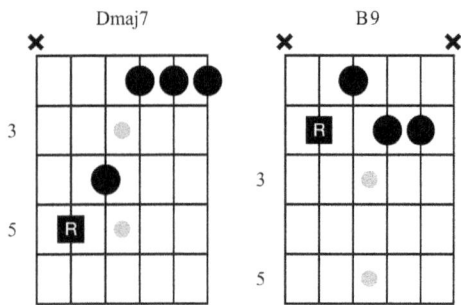

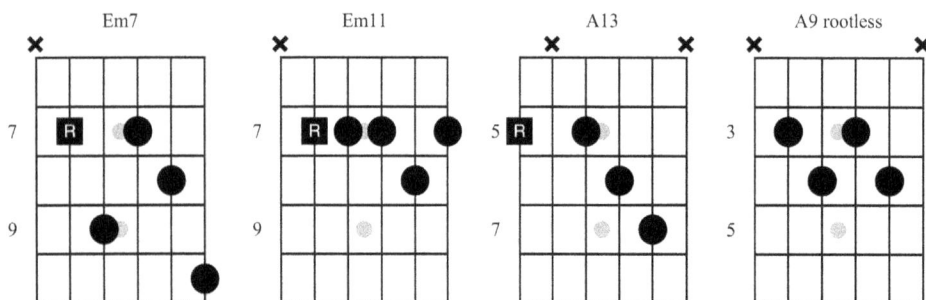

5. ii V transposed up a minor third substitution

Another common bebop device is to take a short harmonic or melodic sequence and transpose it up a minor third – a distance of three frets on the guitar. To incorporate this idea into a ii V I sequence, the ii V cadences are played in half the normal time, so they occupy one bar each.

The progression:

| Em7 A7 | Gm7 C7 | Dmaj7 | |Dmaj7 B7 |

The chord shapes:

Here's a chord shape sequence using this substitution that repeatedly descends from high to low for each chord.

Example 5j

Gm7 Gm11 C13 C9 rootless

Dmaj7 D6(9) Dmaj7 D6(9)

Dmaj7 B7b9(#11)

Em7 Em11 A13 A9 no root Gm7 Gm11 C13 C9 no root

Dmaj7 D6(9) Dmaj7 D6(9) Dmaj7 B7♭9(#11)

Example 5k demonstrates how you might use the minor third substitution in a chord phrase.

Example 5k

6. "Lady Bird" b5 major seventh substitution

Let's look at one final, radical take on our ii V I sequence. *Lady Bird* is a popular jazz standard written way back in 1939 by pianist and composer Tad Dameron. The *Lady Bird* sequence is actually a I vi ii V in C Major, but we'll transpose it to stay in the key of D Major.

I vi ii V in the key of D Major is: Dmaj7 – Bm7 – Em7 – A7

Dameron altered the changes to transform all the chords into major 7ths by substituting the vi ii and V chords. The table below illustrates the logical steps he took to get there.

Original	Dmaj7	Bm7	Em7	A7
Change to dominant	Dmaj7	B7	E7	A7
Tritone substitution	Dmaj7	F7	Bb7	Eb7
Change to major 7ths	Dmaj7	Fmaj7	Bbmaj7	Ebmaj7

Applied to our progression, we can play:

The progression:

| Em7 | A7 | Dmaj7 Fmaj7 | Bbmaj7 Ebmaj7 |

I've purposely not resolved to Dmaj7 at the end, to keep the 4-bar pattern we are working with. The Ebmaj7 chord could resolve to Dmaj7, but equally could lead to another Em7 if the progression is repeated.

The chord shapes:

Now here is a way to play through this sequence that arranges the chords using only the top four strings to keep things light and spacious sounding.

Example 5l

Finally, here is a final chord phrase example which draws ideas from this sequence.

Example 5m

Hopefully this chapter has inspired you to approach the standard ii V I sequence more creatively. I've shown you a few routes through each of the substitution sequences, but of course there are endless combinations available. Set aside practice time over coming weeks and months to explore as many as you can think of using the chord shape sets in Chapter Two.

Chapter Six – Transposing to Other Keys & Progressions

Until now, we've worked exclusively in the key of D Major. It's helpful to apply new ideas and techniques to one key for a while, in order to have a clear view of where we began and where we are now. Now, however, it's time to explore other keys. In this chapter we will…

- Play ii V I sequences in a couple of popular jazz keys

- Map the fretboard with chord shapes in the new key

- Learn melodic chord phrase examples in the new key

Space doesn't allow me to cover too many keys, so I've focused on a few essentials: the keys of F Major and Bb Major, a modal tune in C minor, and a Bb blues progression which incorporates some substitution ideas. All these keys are very popular in jazz.

The Key of F Major

There are a number of great jazz standards written in the key of F Major. Have a listen to:

The Nearness of You

Have You Met Miss Jones

Polka Dots and Moonbeams

Girl from Ipanema

Embraceable You

Georgia

Below I have mapped out the chord shapes for the ii (G minor), V (C Dominant) and I (F Major) chords. Your task is to:

- Play through all of the shape sets

- Combine them in zones on the neck to play ii V I's

- Work out vertical patterns that span the fretboard

- Compose some chord phrases

My advice to you is to embrace what each new key has to offer. Certain combinations will sound great in one key and not so good in another. This can be down to the area of the neck where you're playing, how the chords resonate and whether open strings can be brought into play. Experiment and allow your ears to tell you what sounds good!

Here are the chord shapes:

G minor chord shapes:

Example 6a

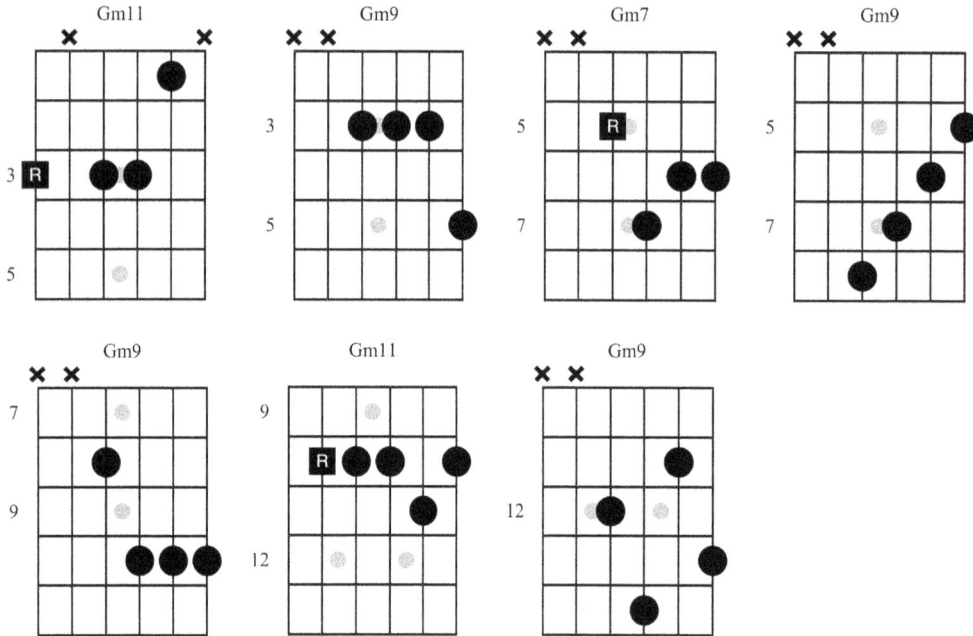

C Dominant chord shapes:

Example 6b

F Major chord shapes:

Example 6c

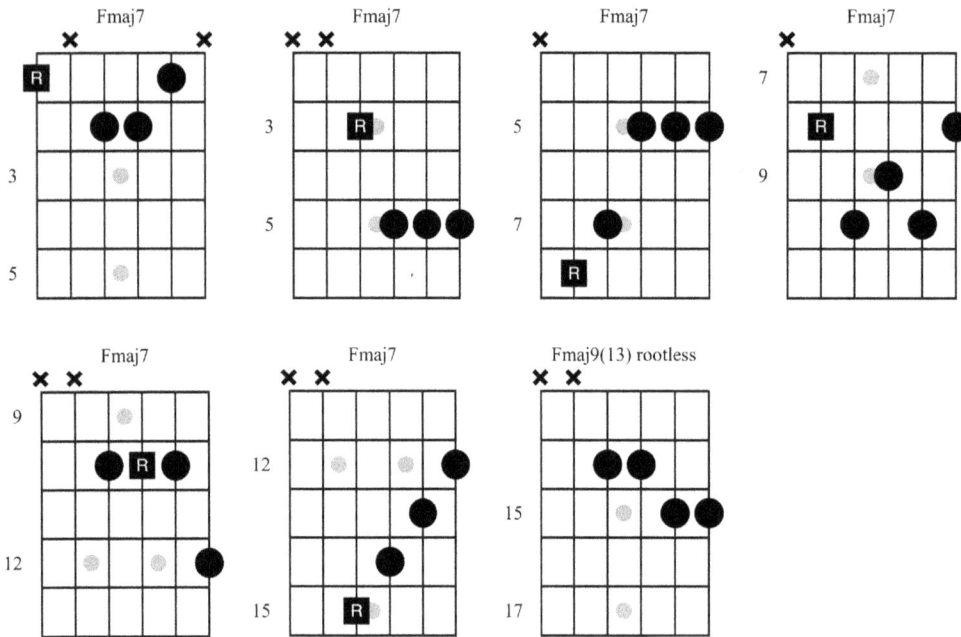

Once you are comfortable with the location of the chord shapes on the neck, it's time to compose some chord phrases that combine multiple voicings. Here are a couple of examples to start you off.

Example 6d

Example 6e

The Key of Bb Major

Popular jazz standards in the key of Bb Major include:

Someday My Prince Will Come

I Got Rhythm (Anthropology, Dexterity, all rhythm changes tunes)

Doxy

Freddie Freeloader

My Foolish Heart

Below are the chord shapes for the ii (C minor), V (F7) and I (Bb Major) chords.

C minor chord shapes:

Example 6f:

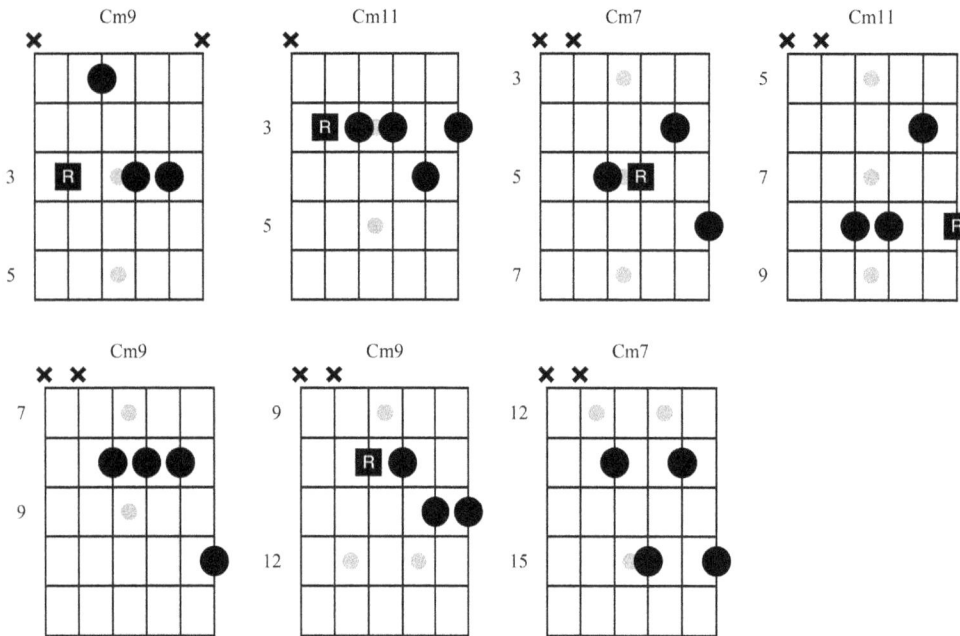

F Dominant chord shapes:

Example 6g

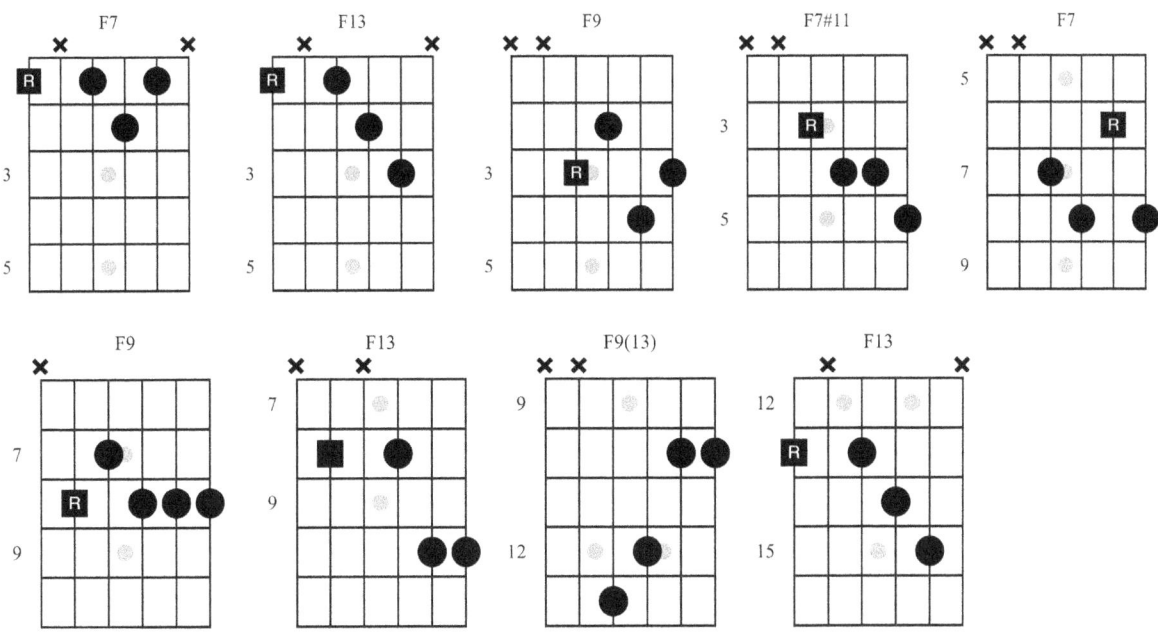

Bb Major chord shapes:

Example 6h

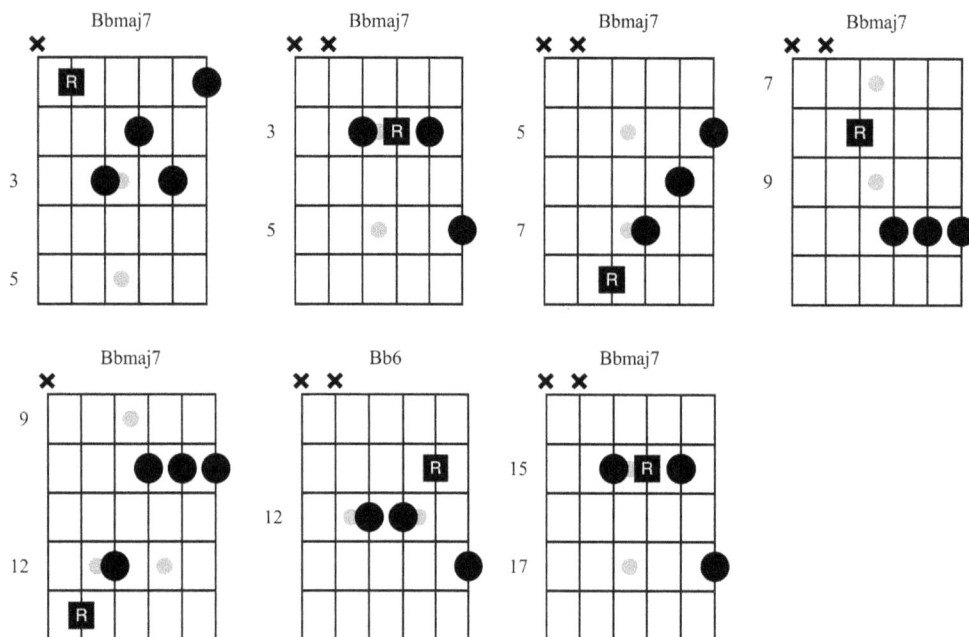

No, here are some chord phrase ideas in Bb Major.

Example 6i

Example 6j

C minor modal tune

Now we're going to take a look at how we might apply vertical chord playing to a modal tune in C minor. It's a simple three-chord harmony, consisting of C minor, F minor and G Altered Dominant.

We've already mapped out a set of C minor shapes, and it's perfectly fine to use those. But, for darker sounding modal tunes (such as Wayne Shorter's *Footprints*) which use the aforementioned three chords, I like to have another tool at my disposal: *quartal voicings*.

Quartal voicings have a cool, unresolved, slightly tense sound. "Quartal" simply means 4ths. We normally build our chord voicings from stacked thirds, but here we build them from stacked fourths.

When soloing over a modal tune like *Footprints,* Miles Davis' *So What*, or John Coltrane's *Impressions*, all of which have long periods of a single minor chord, we would often reach for the Dorian mode which fits the cool vibe beautifully. I like to harmonise the Dorian mode to produce a set of quartal voicings that span the neck.

The C Dorian scale (mode 2 in the key of Bb Major) is constructed from the notes:

C D Eb F G A Bb

If we begin on C and take every fourth note to create a four-note chord voicing we get C, F, Bb and E. Arranged on the guitar neck, this forms a Cm11 chord.

Go to the next note in the scale (D) and repeat the process and we get D, G, C and F. On the guitar, this forms a Dm11 chord.

The third chord is built from Eb and contains the notes Eb, A, C and G, which forms Ebmaj#11, and so on.

The chord grids below show the full set of chords including the C chord an octave higher. Although we can attribute chord names to these shapes, I don't think that's helpful when improvising over a tune in the key of C minor. I just think of these as "C minor chord shape options" that can be played over long modal vamps. (You can transpose these chord shapes up a tone to D minor and practise them over a backing track with the *So What* changes).

Here is the whole set of chord shapes:

Example 6k

Cm11 | Dm11 | Ebmaj7(#11) | F11 | Gm11

Am11 | Bbmaj11 | Cm11

Next we have a set of vertical F minor chords.

F minor chord shapes:

Example 6l

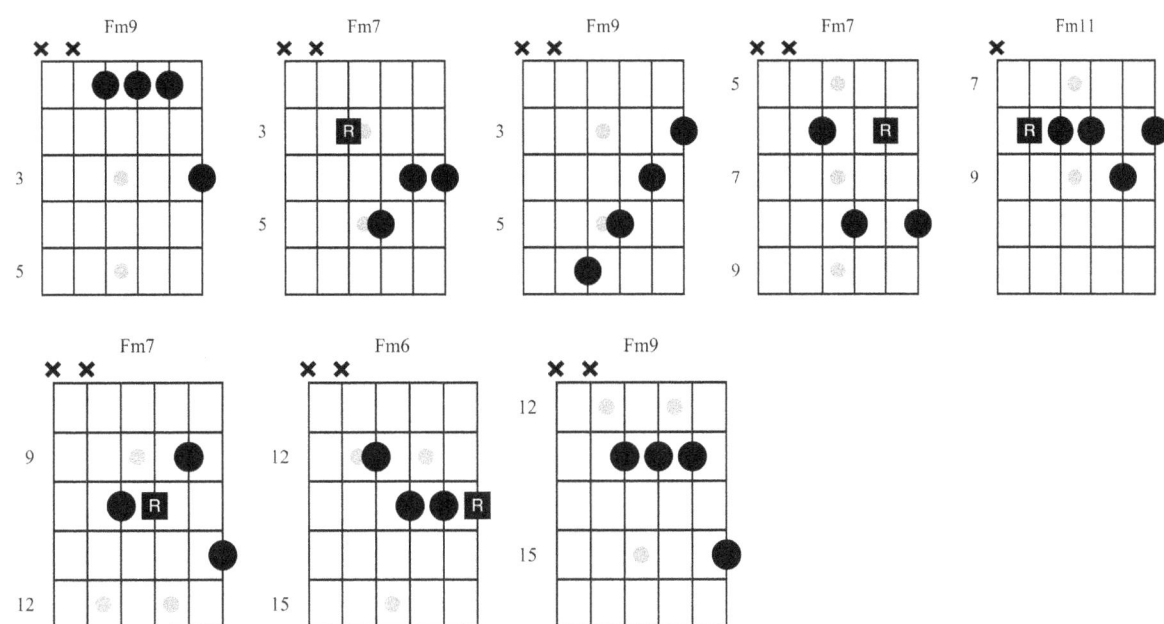

And to complete the set, here are the G dominant chord shapes.

NB: in the key of C minor, chord V is G minor, but typically in a modal tune or minor blues, it is altered to a dominant chord to increase the tension and release when it resolves to the I chord. Occasionally I've opted for a straight G13 chord as it sounded better and fitted more comfortably into the vertical sequence.

G Altered Dominant chord shapes:

Example 6m

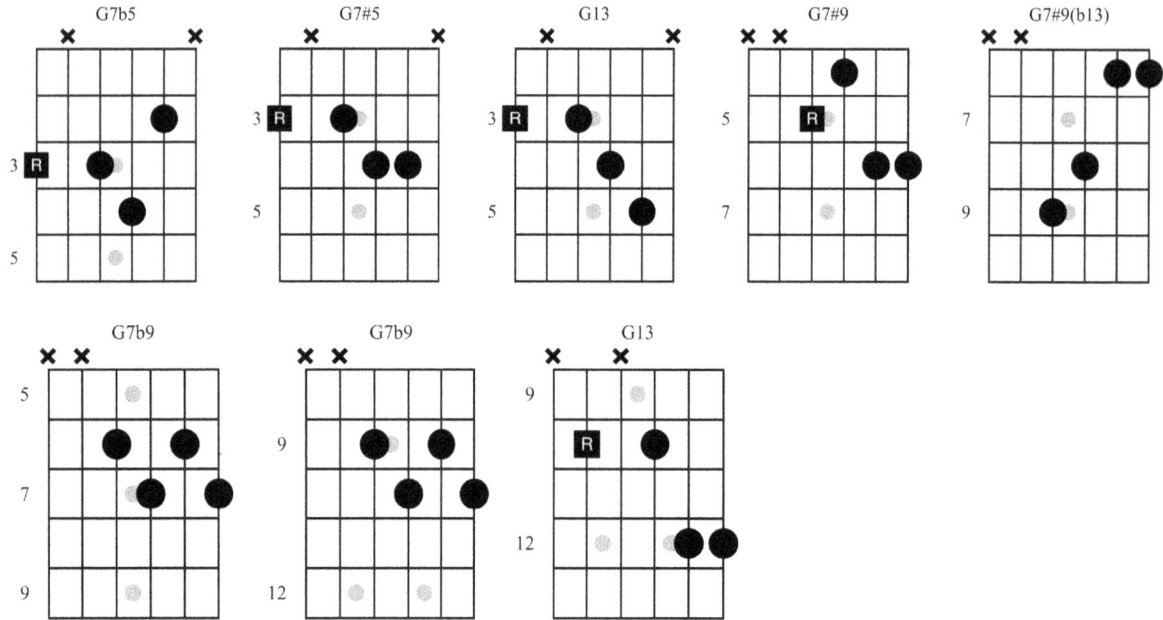

You can use these chord sets to play over tunes like *Blue Bossa* and, of course, *Footprints*. Here is a chord phrase idea using just the C minor chord shapes. In the final chapter you'll learn a comping scheme to play over the whole tune.

Example 6n

Bb Blues

It's always helpful to apply new concepts to a blues – the staple of jam sessions and the format over which so many of us learned to improvise. Below I've provided vertical chord shapes for the basic three-chord blues. As well as the standard chord shapes, however, I've included a set of minor chord shapes.

Back in Chapter One we discussed the concept of substituting rootless chords from different tonalities. We found that by viewing the intervals differently, one stack of notes could be interpreted as major, minor or dominant, depending on the context.

Here is a cool blues substitution idea based on this concept. For any dominant chord, you can substitute chords from the minor tonality a 5th above it. In the case of Bb dominant, this means we can use rootless F minor chords. This idea has been used to great effect by many luminaries of jazz guitar, but none more so than Wes Montgomery and Pat Martino.

So, why does it work?

It's simply due to common notes (illustrated below) and thinking of the intervals differently. The act of *thinking* F minor when playing over a Bb dominant chord, however, is what helps us to quickly access the familiar chord shapes.

Let's take a Bb13 chord – commonly played as chord I in a jazz blues. It is constructed as follows:

Bb13	Bb	D	F	Ab	C	Eb	G
Intervals	Root	3rd	5th	7th	9th	11th	13th

The next table shows the effect of superimposing an Fm7 chord onto Bb13. The first row indicates the notes that form the Fm7 chord. The second row shows the intervals of Fm7. The third row shows which intervals are highlighted when superimposed over a Bb13 chord.

Fm7	F	Ab	C	Eb
Fm7 intervals	Root	3rd	5th	7th
Bb13 intervals	5th	7th	9th	11th

An Fm9 chord superimposed over Bb13 adds another colourful note:

Fm9	F	Ab	C	Eb	G
Fm9 intervals	Root	3rd	5th	7th	9th
Bb13 intervals	5th	7th	9th	11th	13th

If we apply this thinking to the entire blues progression, and substitute chords from the minor tonality a fifth above each one, we get:

Bb dominant = F minor

Eb dominant = Bb minor

F dominant = C minor

In practice this means we now have *six sets* of chord shapes to work with instead of three. We can move freely between the dominant and minor voicings and suddenly we have many more creative options. In terms of playing vertically to span the entire neck, we can fill every "gap".

Important Caveat! This concept works beautifully with small chord voicings – ideally rootless versions. Chord voicings with a root are fine if arranged on the top four strings. Just don't go playing, for instance, a heavy sounding F minor bar chord in position one!

The best way to understand this concept is to hear it in action. Listen to Wes Montgomery's track *Cariba* from the album *Full House*. This is a Bb blues, but the melody is made from Fm7 voicings. When the progression changes to Eb7, Wes plays Bb minor voicings, and so on.

With the audio download of this book I've included a Bb blues with just drums and walking bass. This is for you to comp over to test out these ideas. Your assignment is to:

• Play the blues progression using dominant chord shapes only

• Play the progression using dominant chords and introduce one or two minor chord substitutions

• Play the progression using only minor chord shapes

• Mix and match both sets of shapes to your taste

Remember there are *two sets* of chord shapes you can use for each chord in the standard blues progression. We've already covered some of these chords earlier, so I won't repeat them here. I have just mapped out the new shapes that you need.

Bb Dominant chord shapes:

Example 60

Now refer to the F minor chord shapes from Example 61.

Eb Dominant chord shapes:

Example 6p

The minor tonality a 5th above Eb dominant is Bb minor. Here are the chord shapes.

Bb minor chord shapes:

Example 6q

The V chord of the blues in Bb Major is F7. We have already mapped out the vertical chord shapes for F7 in Example 6g above. We also have the C minor shapes. Example 6f shows the "regular" shapes and Example 6k shows the quartal voicings. You can use the quartal shapes here too!

Refer to all of these shapes as you practise comping over the whole blues progression.

Example 6r shows how you might use a selection of these shapes to comp through two choruses of a Bb blues. Being able to switch between dominant and minor chord shapes opens up many more options. At first it may take you a while to visualise the minor counterparts of the chords in front of you, but after practice, it will become second nature and you'll switch between them at will.

I've deliberately left off the chord names in the following example. Refer back to the relevant chord sets and see if you can identify the chords being used. It's a mix of the original dominant chords, minor substitutions a 5th above, and a few quartal voicings.

Example 6r

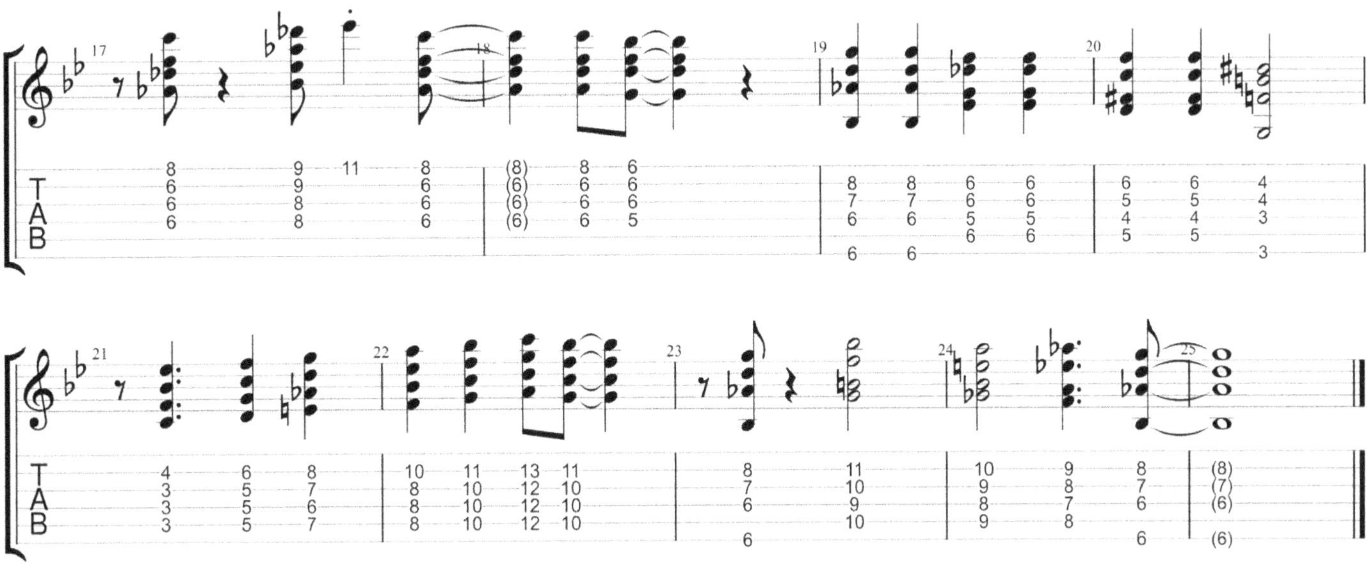

Chapter Seven – Mapping the Minor ii V I

Until now we have worked with the ubiquitous major ii V I sequence. In order to give you a complete set of tools you can use to tackle any jazz standard, in this chapter we will map out *one* minor ii V I sequence. In the final chapter, we'll explore how to apply creative chord thinking to the familiar changes of *Autumn Leaves*, which contains both of these sequences.

The examples in this chapter will be in the key of D minor, so our ii V I progression will be:

Em7b5 – A7 – Dm7

Strictly speaking, the minor ii V I progression, derived from the Harmonic Minor scale, should be written:

Em7b5 – A7alt – Dm(maj7)

You'll occasionally hear this in tunes such as Horace Silver's *Nica's Dream,* for example, but the majority of jazz standards have an "imperfect" ii V I that ends with a straight minor chord (such as in *Autumn Leaves*).

Side note: Jazz composers like the element of surprise, so a number of standards contain minor ii Vs that end with a major rather than minor chord. Check out *How High the Moon* and *Stella by Starlight*, for example. For a comprehensive guide to the minor ii V I progression, there is no better resource than Joseph Alexander's book *Minor ii V I Mastery*.

Mapping the minor ii V I

By now, you should be getting used to the process of taking one chord and mapping it across the fretboard. We'll follow the same method as previously. Your task is to:

- Play through all the chord shape sets

- Combine them in zones on the neck to play ii V I's

- Work out some vertical patterns that span the fretboard

- Compose some chord phrases

As before, I'll provide some examples to get you started. First, play through the following shapes for the Em7b5 chord.

Em7b5 chord shapes:

Example 7a

We've worked on A dominant chord shapes before, but here are a set of shapes specially selected to pair well with m7b5 chords.

A dominant chord shapes:

Example 7b

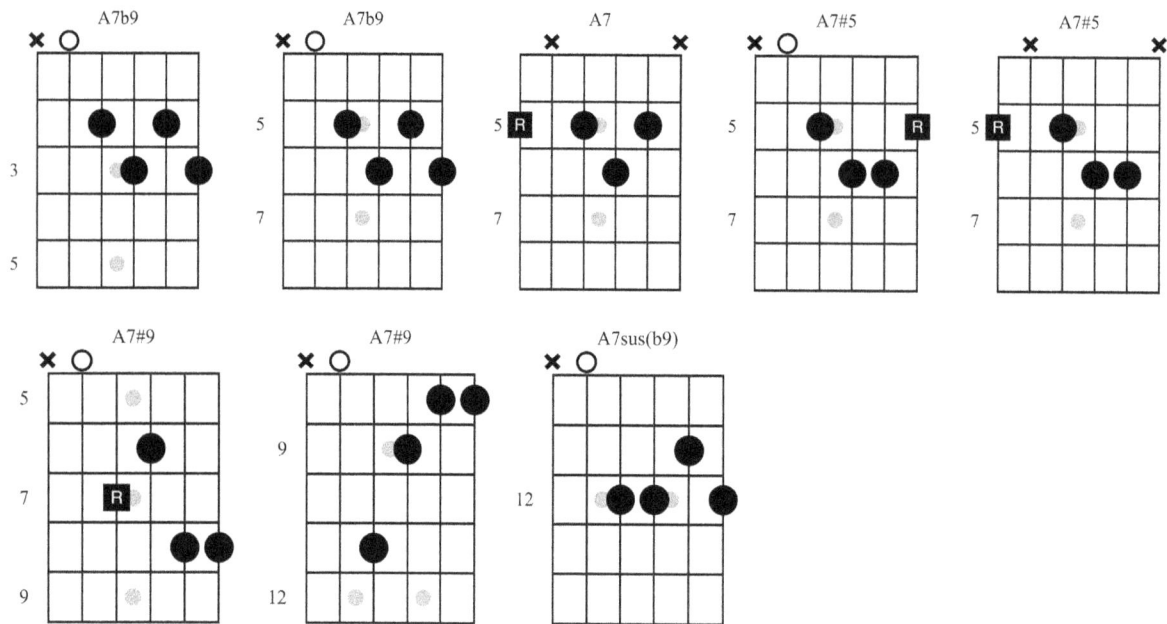

Finally, here are a set of D minor chord shapes to complement the ii V shapes above.

D minor chord shapes:

Example 7c

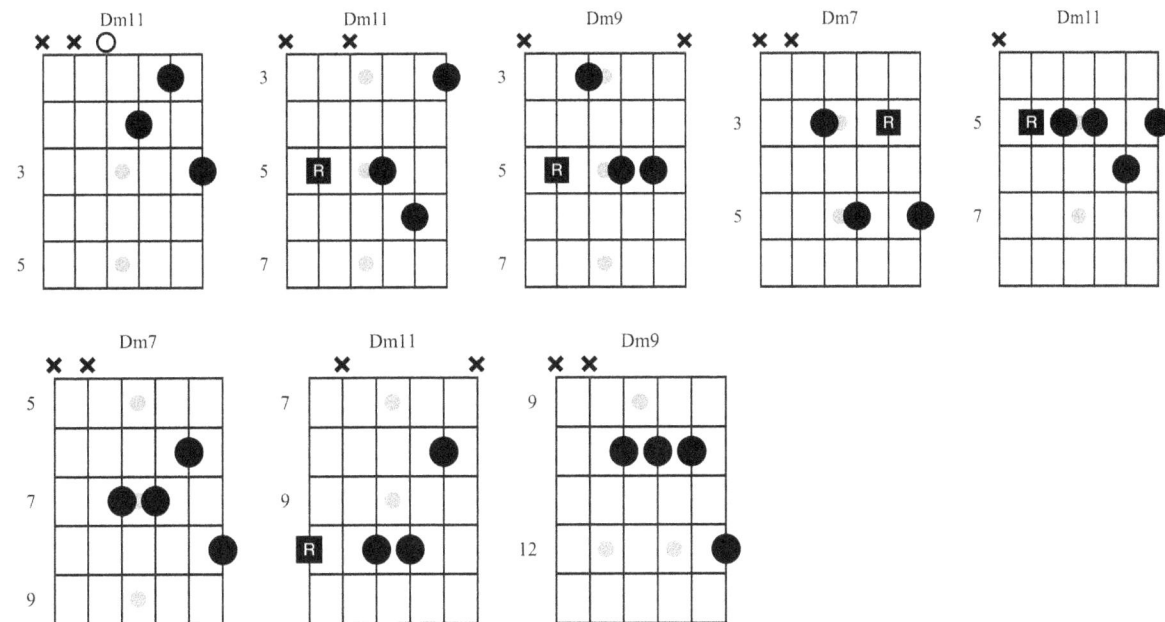

Here are a few examples of how you might combine these chord shapes into pleasing vertical chord patterns playing the minor ii V I sequence.

Example 7d

Em7♭5   Em7♭5   A7   A7♯5

```
T   8       6           5           5
A   7       7           5           6
B   7       7           5           6
                        5           5
                                    0
```

Dm11   Dm7   Dm11

```
T   5       8           3
A   6       6           6
B   5       7           5
    5       7
    5                   5
```

Example 7e

Em7♭5   Em7♭5   A7♯9   A7sus(♭9)

```
T   3       5           8           12
A   3       5           8           11
B   3       5           6           12
    2       5           7           12
                        0           0
```

Dm9   Dm7   Dm11

```
T   12      8           5
A   10      6           6
B   10      7           5
    0       7           5
                        5
```

Example 7f

Example 7g

This has been a very brief look at the minor ii V I, but apply all you've learnt so far and experiment with the minor ii V I in different keys.

Chapter Eight – Applying Chord Creativity to a Jazz Standard

I trust that the ground we've covered so far has added to your practical knowledge of chord voicings and expanded the options at your disposal when comping. We've been on a journey to break out of the rut of playing in "safe areas" of the fretboard. From this point forward, it's all about applying what you've learnt to the music you love. If you put in the work to master your favourite jazz standards, it will pay dividends in all aspects of your playing.

In this chapter I'll give you schemes for playing the changes of two great jazz standards: *Autumn Leaves* and a version of the modal tune *Footprints*. The first has more chord changes, so we'll thoughtfully apply what we've learnt to create a pleasing chordal arrangement. The latter has multiple bars of single chords, so here we can explore how to be creative with chord vamps to create interest and momentum.

How to apply the technique to any chord progression

When you come to apply vertical chord mapping to one of your favourite tunes, refer back to the material we've already covered and follow this method:

- First identify any ii V I sequences in the tune

- Refer to the chord shape sets covered in chapters two and seven.

- Transpose them to the right key for your tune and begin to create vertical chord sequences using the shapes. It will help to write down your own chord grids. Remember that the chord shapes form a *repeating* sequence, so for each chord begin by finding the *lowest playable voicing* on the fretboard and work upwards.

- Practise playing the ii V I sequences in different zones on the neck

- Now work out some vertical sequences that use multiple shapes for one or all of the chords

- Finally, experiment to create some chord phrases you can use as an accompaniment or to play a chord-based solo

Autumn Leaves changes

This is a tune of two distinct halves, made from major and minor ii V Is, which cleverly loops itself around to return to the beginning. I'll call the first half the "A section" and second half the "B section". Below I've mapped out two different ways to play the A section and one way to play the B section. The diagrams below show every chord you'll play in order, so first of all play through them in free time.

A Section – version 1

Here's how these chords sound against a backing track. (A bass and drums backing track is included in the audio download for you to practise along to).

Example 8a

I arranged these chord voicings so that it's possible to play a melodic line around them. Now they can become useful for chord-melody soloing. This is quite a simple example for the purpose of illustration, and you should experiment to see what alternative chord phrases you can come up with. I recommend playing in free time to begin with, and when you've formulated some good ideas, try playing them to tempo.

Example 8b

A Section – version 2

Now try a more adventurous take on comping through the changes – one which uses the full range of the fretboard and more chords per beat. Think of this as an exercise to help you explore the many possible ways of navigating the changes. Your bandmates may not necessarily thank you for playing a chord on every beat (you already know that less is more!) but it's helpful to see what can be put in before you decide what to leave out.

Example 8c

B Section

Now let's turn our attention to the B section of the tune. It begins with a minor ii V I then moves through the changes to resolve nicely to the A section.

For this section I opted to use more open-sounding 7b9 chord shapes. Due to their moveable nature, they are a gift when it comes to arranging tunes.

You'll notice the inclusion of the dark sounding Gmaj7#11 chord in bar 4. This seems like a curve ball, given that the chord in the original changes here is an Fm7, but it can be explained! If you added an E bass note to this chord then it could be viewed as an Em6(9), but when we hit the E minor section of the tune, I was simply thinking about ascending the E minor scale using quartal voicings: Em11 – F#m11 – Gmaj7#11.

In bar 6, the Ab7#9 is a flat five substitution for the D7 chord.

Bars 11 and 12 in the original changes contain two ii V sequences: Em7 – A7 – Dm7 – G7. I've opted to replace the A7 with Ebm11 – a unusual minor b5 substitution, but one which makes perfect sense as it creates a chromatic descending sequence.

Gmaj7#11   Am9   Ab7#9   Gmaj9   Cmaj7   F#m7b5

B7b9   Em11   Ebm11   Dm11   G13   F#m7b5

B7#9   Em9

Example 8d

Now, here are three different ways in which you could comp through the full 32-bar sequence, using many of the techniques we've covered. Try the examples below, then jam along to the backing track and try out your own ideas. Again, I've not written in chord names. You know the basic chord changes. See if you can identify all of the chords being used.

Example 8e

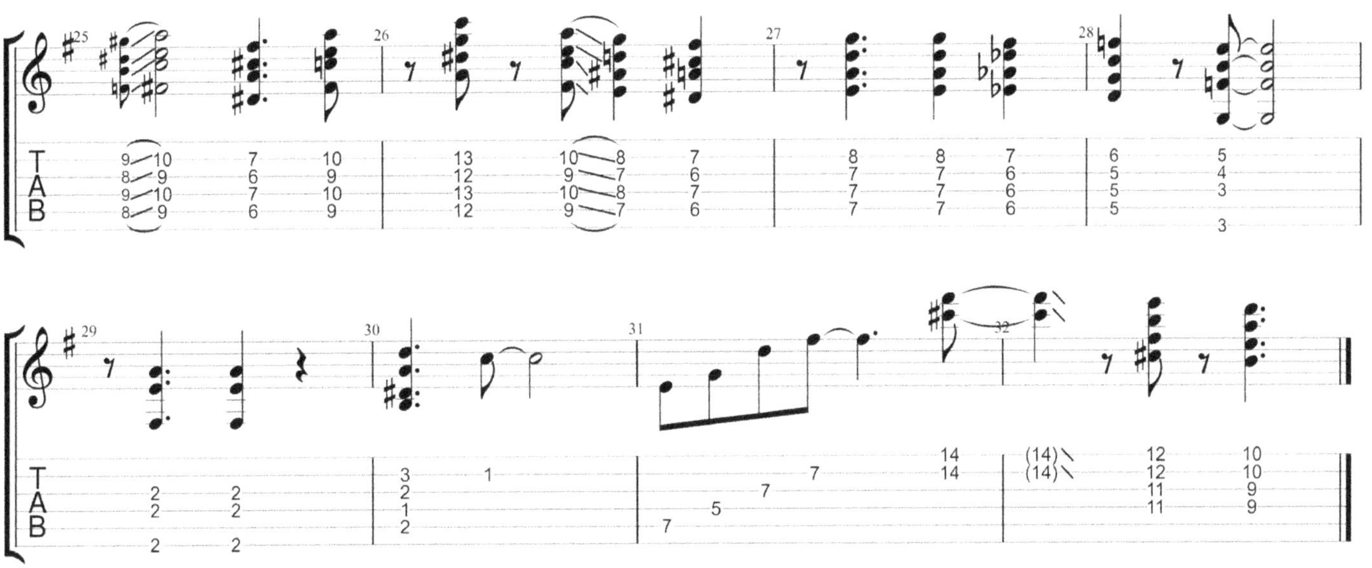

Example 8f

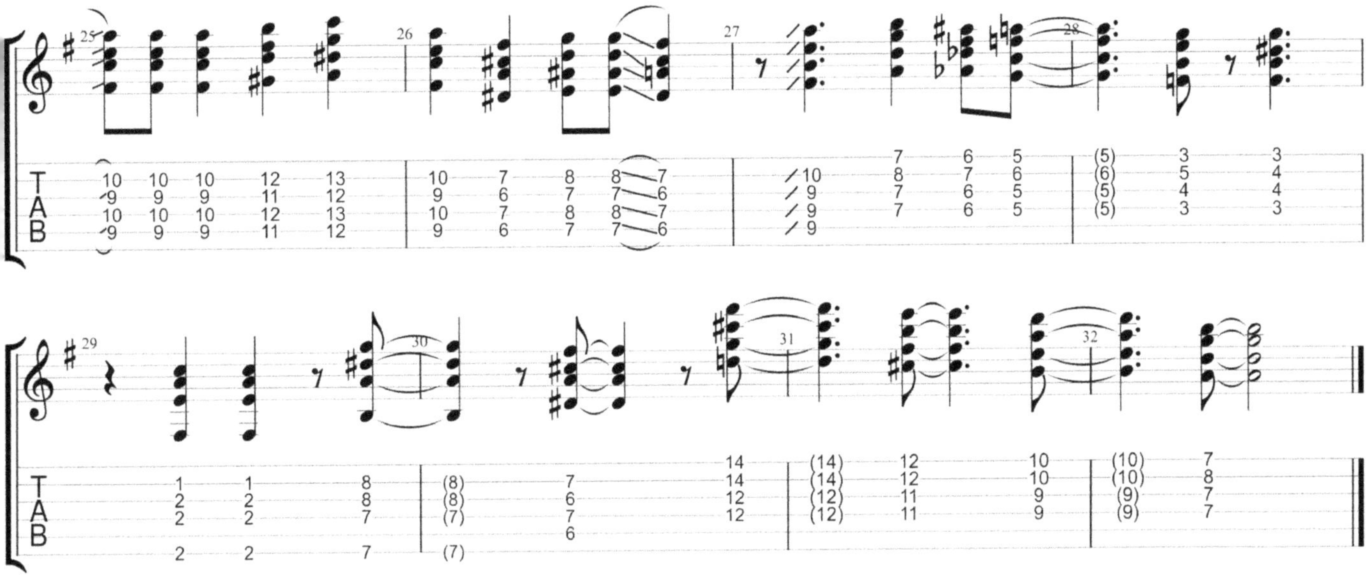
TAB
TAB

Example 8g

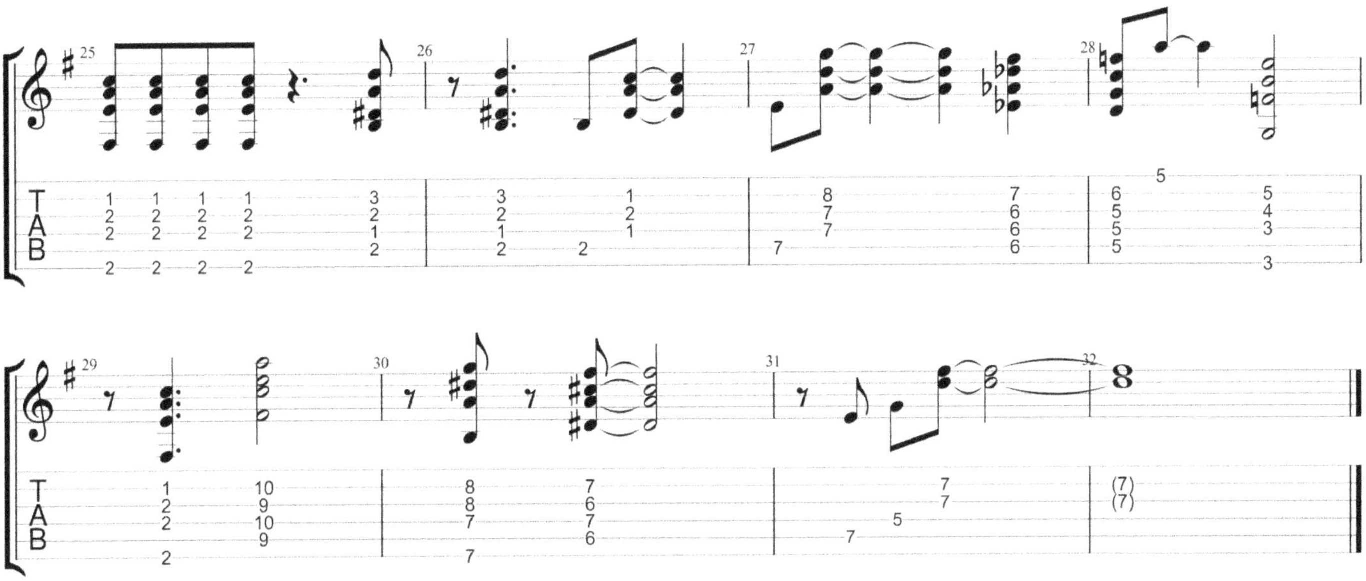

Modal changes

Our modal tune example is loosely based on the chord changes to Wayne Shorter's *Footprints*. There are a few different versions of the ending of this tune in circulation, as different musicians have reharmonized the chords. It's in the key of C minor and I have opted to make the final chord change a G7alt, so that the whole progression can be viewed as a kind of minor blues (albeit one stretched out to 24 bars).

This tune is also in 3/4 time, so it demands a different feel when comping. Below I've played two complete versions of the form. Here's the first:

Example 8g shows how the chord changes sound over the backing track. The chords for the first four bars are all quartal voicings, derived from the C Dorian mode. Once again, don't be confused by the chord names – it's the sound that's important. In bars 19–20 I've used a flat five substitution (Db9 for G7alt) and preceded the substituted dominant chord with its ii chord (Ab minor).

Example 8h

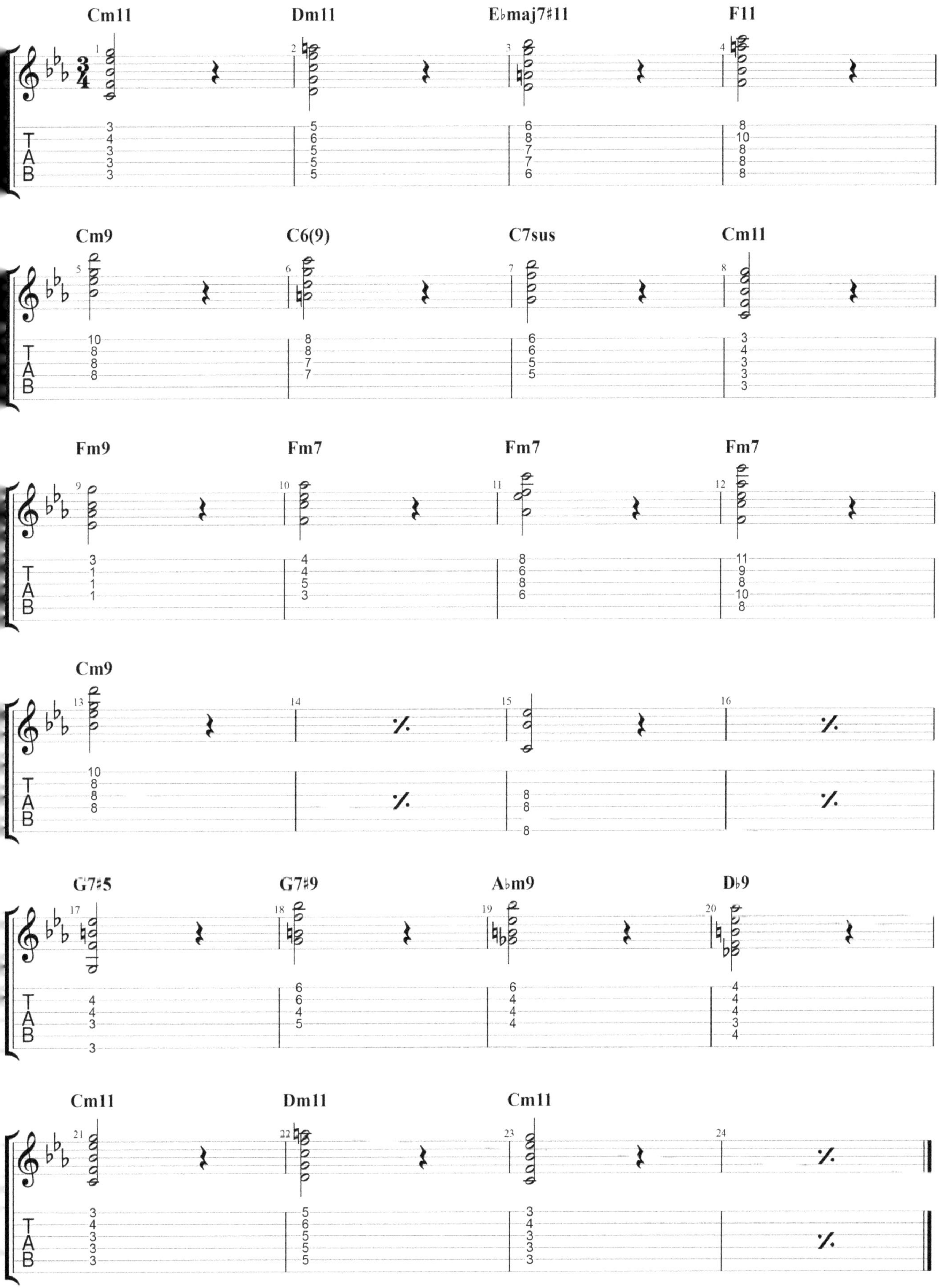
Cm11
Dm11
E♭maj7♯11
F11
Cm9
C6(9)
C7sus
Cm11
Fm9
Fm7
Fm7
Fm7
Cm9
G7♯5
G7♯9
A♭m9
D♭9
Cm11
Dm11
Cm11

Here is a second pass of the progression. In this version I've made extensive use of the same four-note chord on the high E and B strings. The first occurrence is chord three in the sequence below, played in seventh position, which you may recognise as an Am11 chord. Since the bass guitar is vamping on a C note, however, the chord takes on the sound of a C6(9) chord. Each time this chord occurs, it's in a slightly different context. It's a versatile voicing and its ambiguous sound makes it ideal for modal tunes like this. I've also included the maj7 for m9 substitution in this version.

Example 8i

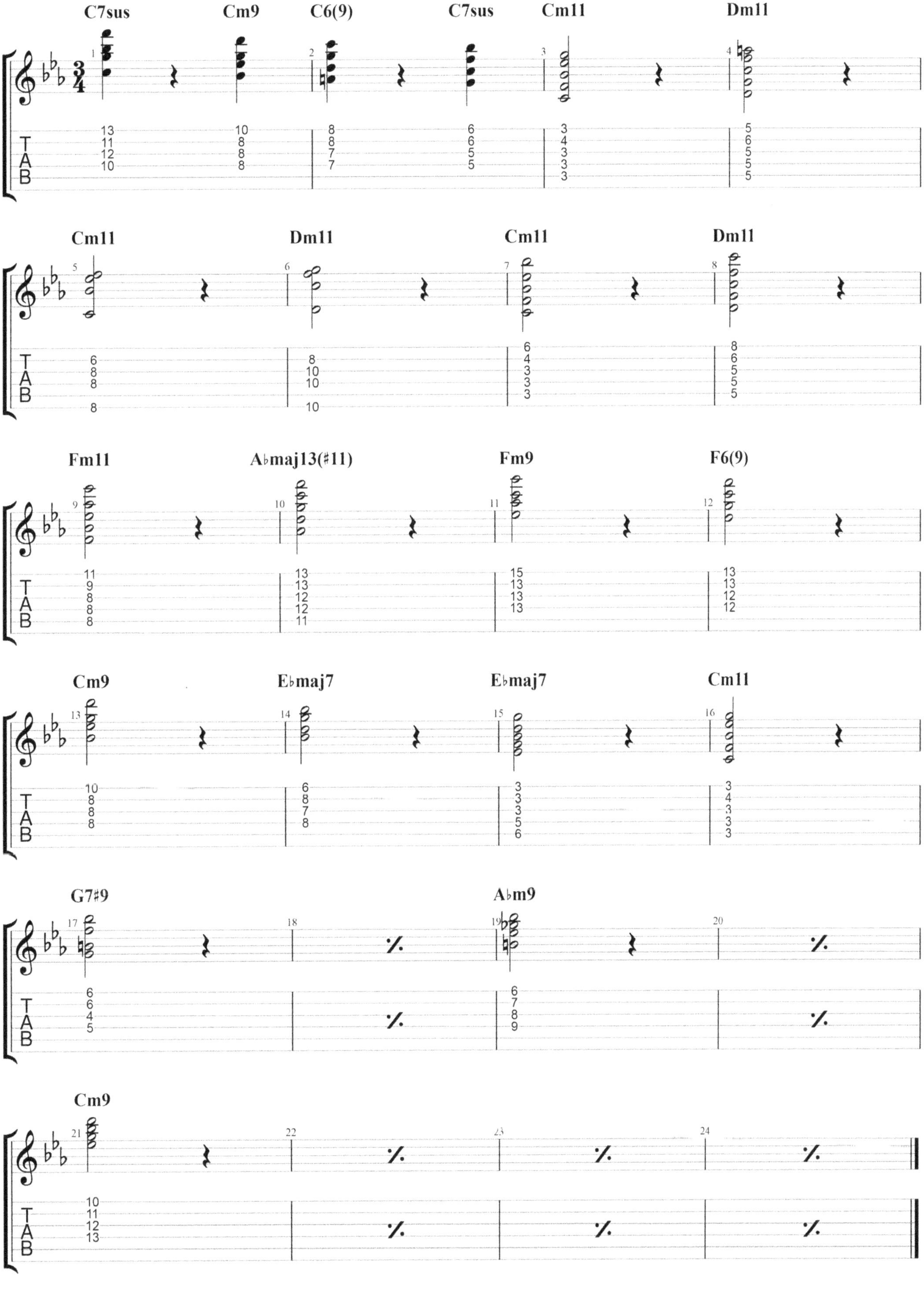
C7sus
Cm9
C6(9)
C7sus
Cm11
Dm11
Cm11
Dm11
Cm11
Dm11
Fm11
A♭maj13(♯11)
Fm9
F6(9)
Cm9
E♭maj7
E♭maj7
Cm11
G7♯9
A♭m9
Cm9

You'll notice that I've not included any chord-phrase examples for this tune. Your job is to use the chord shapes above and work out some of your own. Experiment playing to the backing track and see what ideas you come up with.

Conclusion

If you've worked diligently through the material in this book and incorporated these ideas into your practice regime, you should be well on your way to breaking down the mystery of the fretboard. If you work at combining multiple vertical chord shapes when you comp through a tune, you'll immediately sound more musical. Not only will your harmonic knowledge grow, but you'll begin to compose more interesting melodic lines based around the chord shapes.

Here's a reminder of the method to apply this to your favourite standards:

- First identify any ii V I sequences in the tune

- Refer to the chord shape sets covered in chapters two and seven.

- Transpose them to the right key for your tune and begin to create vertical chord sequences using the shapes. It will help to write down your own chord grids. Remember that the chord shapes form a *repeating* sequence, so for each chord begin by finding the *lowest playable voicing* on the fretboard and work upwards.

- Practise playing the ii V I sequences in different zones on the neck

- Now work out some vertical sequences that use multiple shapes for one or all of the chords

- Finally, experiment to create some chord phrases you can use as an accompaniment or to play a chord-based solo

As always, enjoy your playing and allow yourself the freedom to experiment!

Other Jazz Books From Fundamental Changes

100 Classic Jazz Licks For Guitar

Advanced Jazz Guitar Concepts

Fundamental Changes in Jazz Guitar

Jazz Bebop Blues Guitar

Jazz Blues Soloing for Guitar

Jazz Guitar Chord Mastery

Chord Tone Soloing For Jazz Guitar

Martin Taylor – Walking Bass for Jazz Guitar

Martin Taylor – Beyond Chord Melody

Martin Taylor – Single Note Soloing for Jazz Guitar

Minor ii V Mastery for Jazz Guitar

Modern Jazz Guitar Concepts

Rhythm Changes for Jazz Guitar

The Complete Jazz Guitar Soloing Compilation

The First 100 Jazz Chords for Guitar

The Jazz Guitar Chord Compilation

Voice Leading Jazz Guitar

Scan the QR code with your smartphone to discover more: